ARCTIC OCEAN

Baltic
Sea

EUROPE

ASIA

Black Sea

Sea

PACIFIC

OCEAN

Red Sea

China

Sea

Arabian Sea

AFRICA

INDIAN OCEAN

AUSTRALIA

Tasman

Sea

NEW
ZEALAND

First published in Great Britain 1977 by Ward Lock Limited,
116 Baker Street, London, W1M 2BB,
a Pentos company.

© **Grisewood & Dempsey Limited 1977.**
Reprinted 1980

Designed and produced by Grisewood & Dempsey Limited,
Grosvenor House, 141-143 Drury Lane, London WC2

Printed in Italy by Vallardi Industrie Grafiche, Milan.

ISBN 0 7063 5333 1

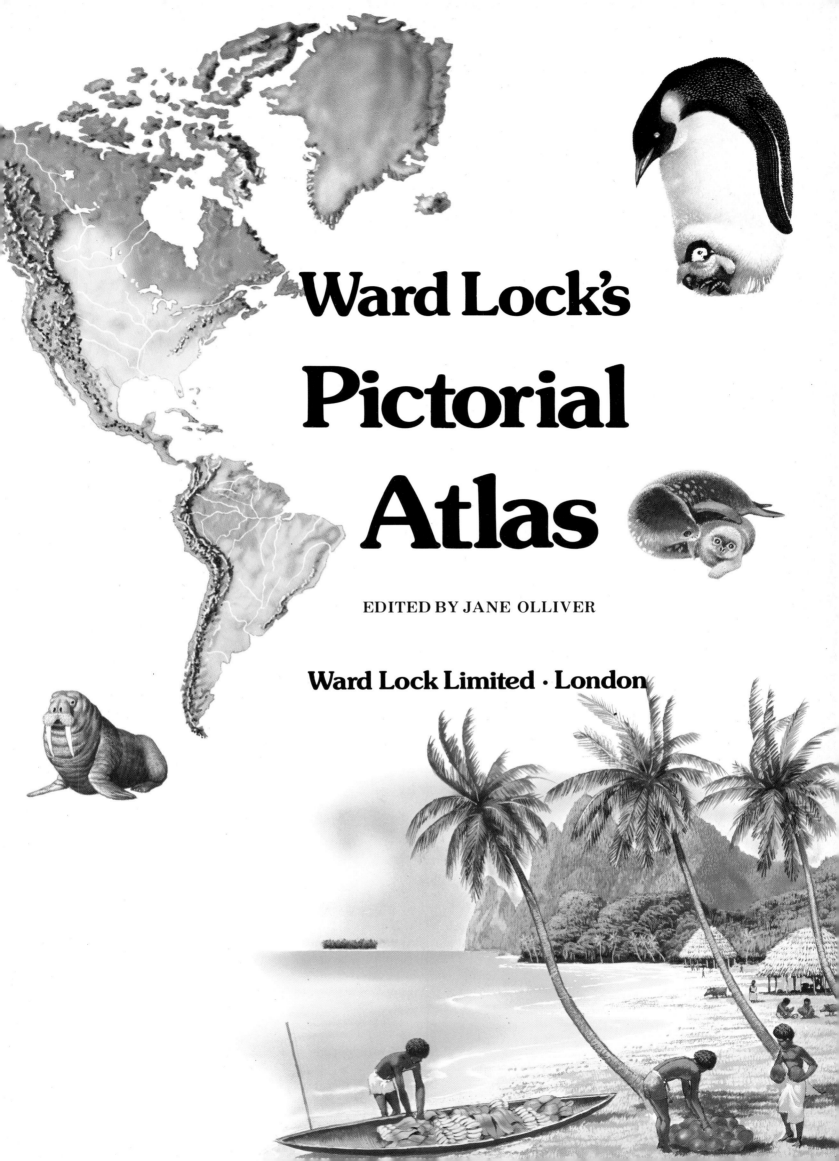

Ward Lock's
Pictorial
Atlas

EDITED BY JANE OLLIVER

Ward Lock Limited · London

Contents

The Earth in Space

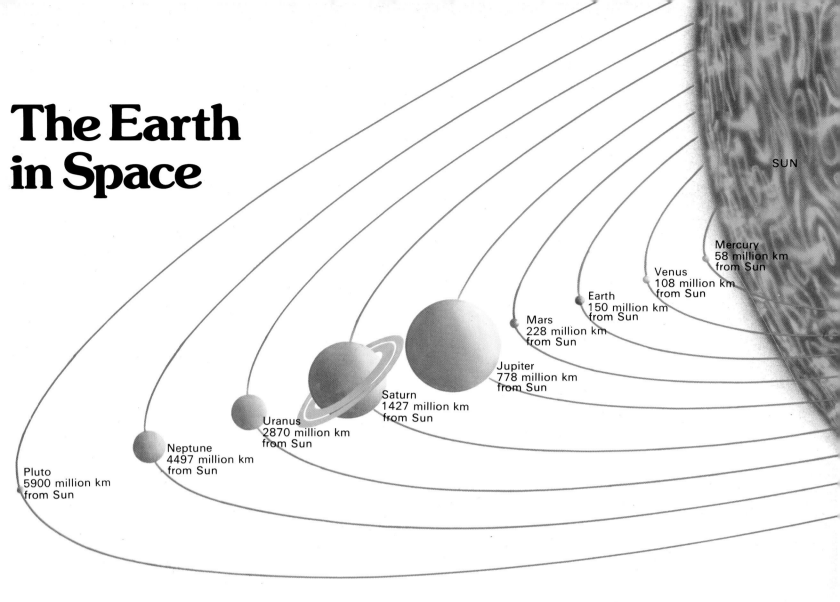

SUN

Mercury
58 million km
from Sun

Venus
108 million km
from Sun

Earth
150 million km
from Sun

Mars
228 million km
from Sun

Jupiter
778 million km
from Sun

Saturn
1427 million km
from Sun

Uranus
2870 million km
from Sun

Neptune
4497 million km
from Sun

Pluto
5900 million km
from Sun

Long ago people believed that the Earth was the centre of the universe and that the Sun and the stars spun around it. Now we know that our Earth is one of nine planets that circle (*orbit*) the Sun.

The Sun with its family of planets, and thousands of smaller bodies called *asteroids*, is known as the *solar system*. The nine planets of the solar system, including the Earth, are Mercury (the smallest planet and nearest to the Sun), Venus, Mars, Jupiter (the largest planet—1300 times bigger than the Earth), Saturn, Uranus, Neptune, and Pluto. Our solar system is part of a vast cluster of stars called a *galaxy*. We see these stars in the sky at night and call them the Milky Way. The Milky Way and thousands of millions of other galaxies make up the universe. The size of the universe is so great that nobody can tell how big it is.

The Earth is not a very large planet but it is the only one known to have living things on it. Life is made possible by the Sun. This huge ball of hot gases gives out heat and light. Without it our world would be dark, frozen, and dead.

The Sun is just one of thousands of millions of stars in the universe. It is not the biggest star, nor is it the brightest. It looks bigger and brighter to us because it is much closer than any other star. The Sun is almost 150 million kilometres from the Earth. The nearest star, Proxima Centauri, is about 42 million million kilometres away. Compared with the Earth, the Sun is gigantic. It is over a million times bigger than our planet.

The solar system is made up of nine planets revolving around the Sun. Their routes are not perfect circles but oval in shape, so their distances from the Sun vary as they orbit. The planets nearest to the Sun take a shorter time to complete an orbit than the ones farther away.

Light from Outer Space

Stars are balls of hot gases that give off their own light. (The Moon is not a star. It reflects the Sun's light.) Stars are so far away that we measure their distances in *light years*. A light year is the distance that light travels in one year (10 million million kilometres). Some of the stars in the sky are so far away that it takes thousands of years for their light to reach us.

The Moon is a satellite of the Earth, just as the Earth is a satellite of the Sun. It circles us every month (27 days 8 hours to be exact). The Moon is our nearest neighbour and so far the only place that people have visited in space. In 1969, the American astronauts, Aldrin and Armstrong, were the first to make a landing on the Moon.

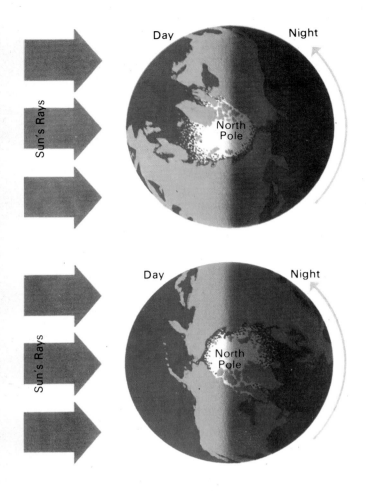

The Planet Earth

The Earth is the fifth largest planet in the solar system and probably the only one on which there is life. Once people thought that the Earth was flat, and sailors dared not sail too far for fear of falling off the edge. We now know that the Earth is the shape of a ball, flattened slightly at the top and bottom. It bulges a little at the *equator*, an imaginary line round its middle.

Some scientists believe that the Earth and the other planets were once part of the Sun. A large star passed close by and caused some of the Sun to break away and form into nine planets. Other scientists think that the Sun and the planets were all formed about the same time—about five thousand million years ago.

At first the Earth was just a ball of red-hot liquid rocks and burning gases. Millions of years later the liquid ball began to cool down. A solid crust began forming on the outside. As the gases cooled, water condensed and formed the oceans. The part of the crust that remained above the water became the continents and islands.

It was many millions of years later that the first living things appeared in the sea. And many more millions of years passed before the first people appeared.

Day and night occur because the Earth spins like a top as it circles the Sun. It takes 24 hours (one day) for the Earth to make one complete spin. Only one half of the world is facing the Sun at any one time. The other half of the Earth is in darkness. Day follows night as the Earth spins towards the east.

It takes $365\frac{1}{4}$ days for the Earth to travel around the Sun. We measure a year as 365 days. The extra quarters make an additional day every four years and we call this a *leap year*. A leap year has 366 days.

The seasons are caused by the tilt of the Earth as it goes round the Sun. Although the Earth moves in a circular path around the Sun, the North and South Poles always point in the same direction in space. So, for part of the year the North Pole tilts towards the Sun (1). This gives the northern hemisphere its summer and the southern hemisphere its winter. Six months (or half an orbit) later, the North Pole is tilted away from the Sun (3) and the seasons are reversed. When the Earth is tilted sideways to the Sun, we have autumn and spring (2 and 4).

Near the equator the tilt of the Earth has little effect. The year there is usually divided into only two seasons—wet and dry.

THE SEASONS

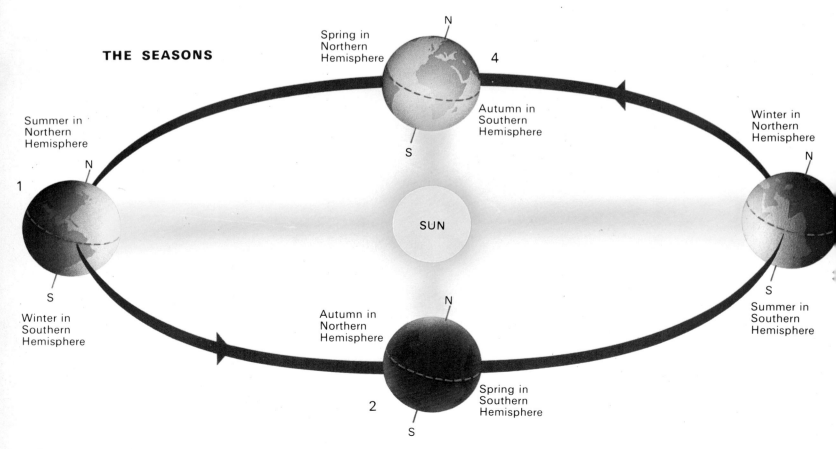

Inside the Earth

The centre of the Earth is called the *core* (made up of the outer and inner core). Here the temperature is so hot (more than 6000°C) that the rocks are liquid. Around the core is the *mantle,* believed to be made of heavy rock which is partly solid. The *crust* is the thin outer layer that includes the land masses and ocean beds.

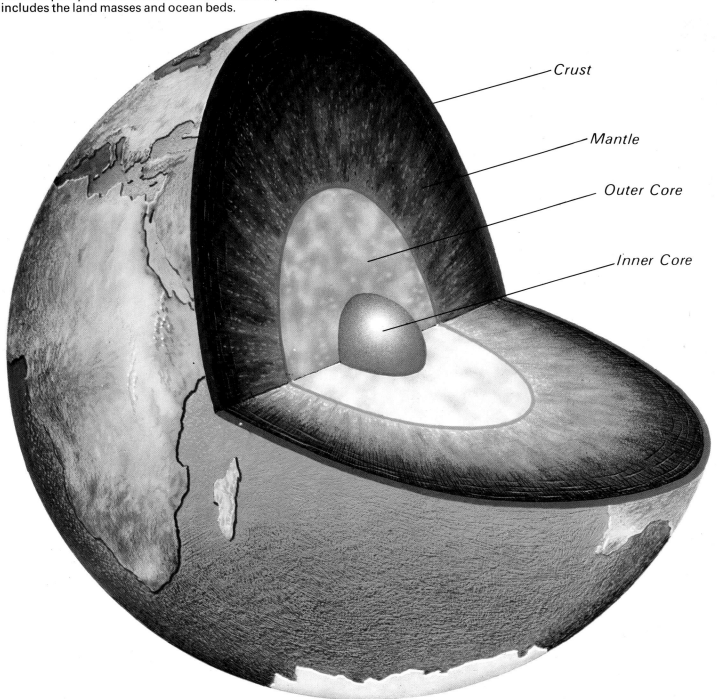

Crust

Mantle

Outer Core

Inner Core

FACTS ABOUT THE EARTH

Diameter at equator : 12,757 km

Diameter at poles : 12,714 km

Circumference at equator : 40,076 km

Circumference at poles : 40,008 km

Approximate distance to centre : 6370 km

Distance from Sun : 149,500,000 km

Distance from Moon : 384,393 km

Weight : 6700 million million million tonnes

Highest point : Mt Everest, Himalayas—8848 m

Lowest point : Mariana Trench, Pacific—11,022 m

Land area : 145,485,000 sq km

Ocean area : 365,320,000 sq km

Average speed in orbit : 0.465 km per second

Angle of tilt : $23\frac{1}{2}$°

The Face of the Earth

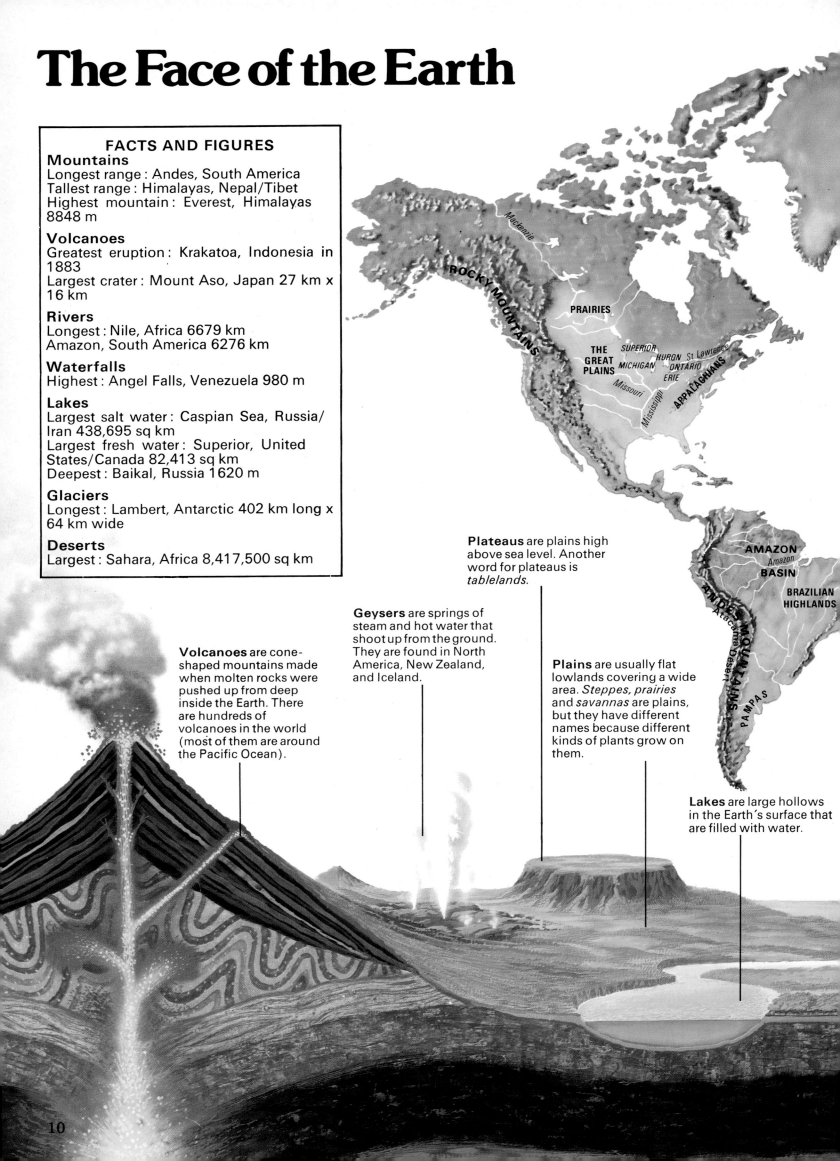

Plateaus are plains high above sea level. Another word for plateaus is *tablelands.*

Geysers are springs of steam and hot water that shoot up from the ground. They are found in North America, New Zealand, and Iceland.

Volcanoes are cone-shaped mountains made when molten rocks were pushed up from deep inside the Earth. There are hundreds of volcanoes in the world (most of them are around the Pacific Ocean).

Plains are usually flat lowlands covering a wide area. *Steppes, prairies* and *savannas* are plains, but they have different names because different kinds of plants grow on them.

Lakes are large hollows in the Earth's surface that are filled with water.

10

Mountains are high
points of land on the
Earth's surface. Much of
the Earth, both on land
and under the sea, is
covered with mountains.
Some undersea
mountains are so high
they reach the surface
and become islands.

Rivers are water-filled
channels that drain the
land. Rain falling on the
ground is carried back to
the sea in rivers.

Deserts are areas of
land so dry that few
plants can survive there.
Deserts are usually found
in the middle of large
continents.

Glaciers are large sheets
of ice that move slowly
down a mountainside or
across the land. As they
move, they scrape away
the surface, sometimes
forming deep valleys.

Waterfalls are created
when a river drops over a
layer of hard rock.

URAL MOUNTAINS

CENTRAL
SIBERIAN PLATEAU

Lena

Yenisei

Ob

Amur

LAKE
BAIKAL

NORTH EUROPEAN PLAIN

Rhine

A L P S

Danube

Dnieper

Volga

Caucasus

CASPIAN
SEA

ARAL
SEA

LAKE
BALKHASH

Gobi
Desert

TIBETAN
PLATEAU

Hwang Ho

Yangtse-Kiang

Mt Everest

HIMALAYAS

ATLAS MTS

S A H A R A

Nile

Arabian
Desert

Indus

Ganges

DECCAN

LAKE CHAD

Niger

ZAIRE
BASIN

Zaire

LAKE
VICTORIA

Zambezi

Kalahari
Desert

Orange

Drakensberg
Mts

Australian
Desert

Land and Sea

Although we call our world 'Earth', most of it is water. Great seas cover almost 70 per cent of its surface. As the seas are joined together, there is really only one big sea in the world. But it has been divided into five main areas called oceans: the Pacific, the Atlantic, the Indian, the Arctic, and the Antarctic. The largest is the Pacific Ocean. It measures 181 million square kilometres. The deepest place in the oceans is 11,022 metres—the Mariana Trench in the Pacific Ocean.

The Earth's land is divided into six continents: Asia, Africa, America, Australia, Antarctica, and Europe. Many people count North America and South America as two separate continents—which would then make seven continents.

The Pacific Ocean stretches from the American coasts in the east to Asia and Australia in the west. From the north it goes from the Bering Sea right down to the Antarctic Ocean in the south. It makes up about half of the water surface of the world.
The picture below shows a coral reef and some of the many different creatures that live in the ocean.

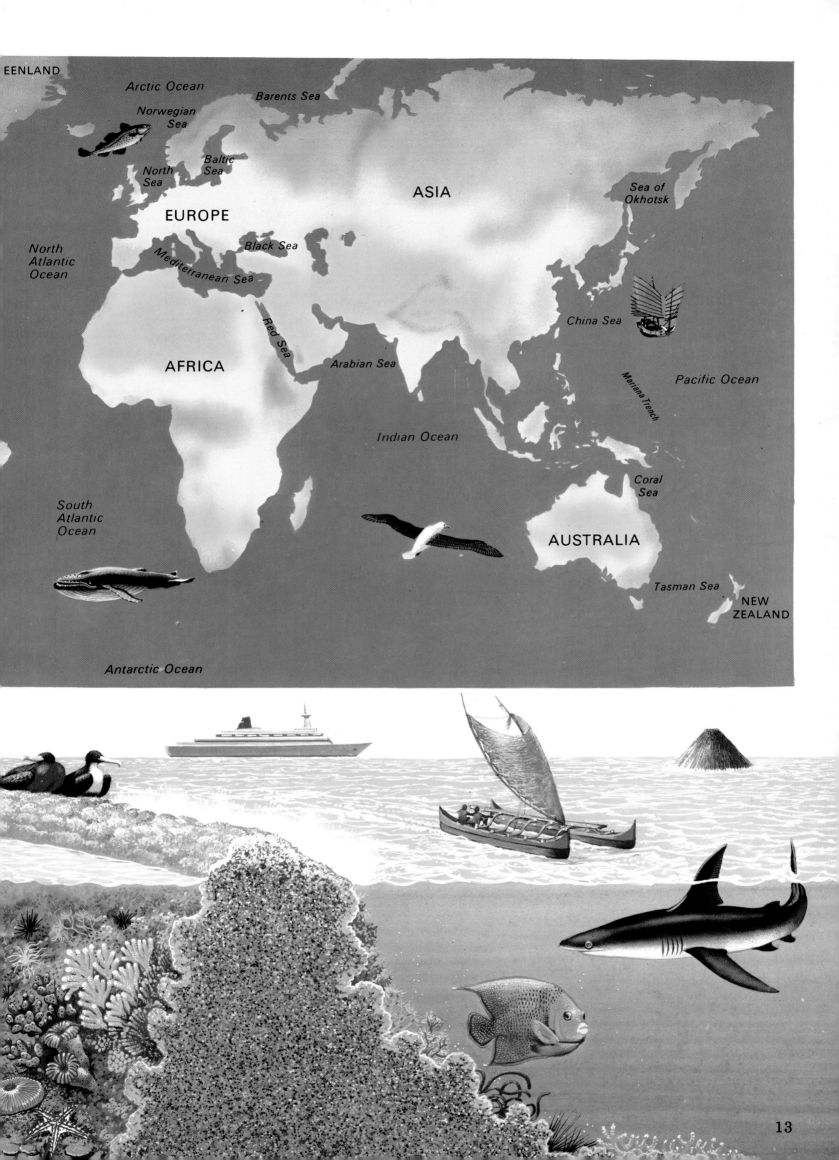

EENLAND

Arctic Ocean

Barents Sea

Norwegian
Sea

Baltic
Sea

North
Sea

ASIA

Sea of
Okhotsk

EUROPE

North
Atlantic
Ocean

Black Sea

Mediterranean Sea

China Sea

Red Sea

AFRICA

Arabian Sea

Mariana Trench

Pacific Ocean

Indian Ocean

Coral
Sea

South
Atlantic
Ocean

AUSTRALIA

Tasman Sea

NEW
ZEALAND

Antarctic Ocean

World Climates

The kind of weather that an area has over a long period of time is called *climate*. In the far north and south it is very cold. It is very hot at the equator. The climate of a region depends on many things. Probably the two most important things are the amount of Sun's heat reaching an area (see diagram on the right), and the nearness of an area to the sea. Water takes longer to warm up than land but it also cools more slowly. And so areas near the sea usually have warmer winters than inland areas because the sea is still warm from the summer. But areas near the coast have cooler summers because the sea takes a long time to warm up after the winter. The sea's currents also carry heat and cold to other regions.

The kinds of plants that grow in an area depend on the climate. The map below shows the main regions of climate and their plant life.

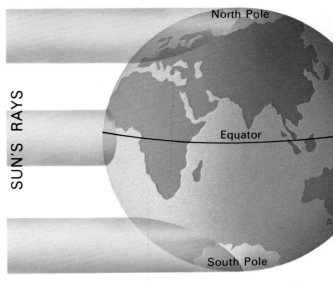

The main thing affecting climate is the amount of heat coming from the Sun. Most heat is received near the equator. The Sun is weaker nearer the poles. Here the rays have to travel farther through the atmosphere and do not fall directly on the Earth's surface.

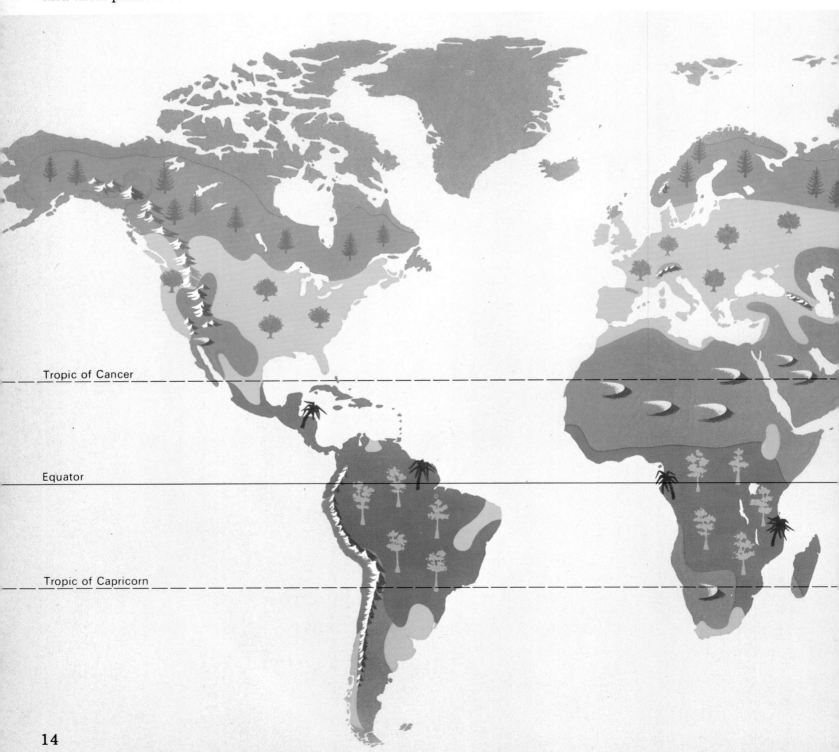

Tropic of Cancer

Equator

Tropic of Capricorn

1 **Polar and mountain climates** are very cold in both summer and winter. Only small hardy plants, such as mosses and lichens, manage to grow in the few places not covered by snow.

 2 **Cold forest climates** have cool summers and long snowy winters. Vast forests of conifers cover the land. These hardy trees can grow in this cold climate. The forests give us much of the timber we use.

 3 **Temperate climates** have warm summers and cool winters. In most places rain falls fairly regularly. But, around the Mediterranean, summers are dry and irrigation is necessary to grow crops.

 4 **Desert climates** are found where there is very little rain. In some places nothing grows, in others just a few low, thorny bushes and palm trees grow up around places where there is water (called *oases*).

 5 **Tropical climates** are found near both sides of the equator. Here it is hot all year and there is neither winter nor summer. Rain may fall all year giving dense forest, but some places have a wet season and a dry season.

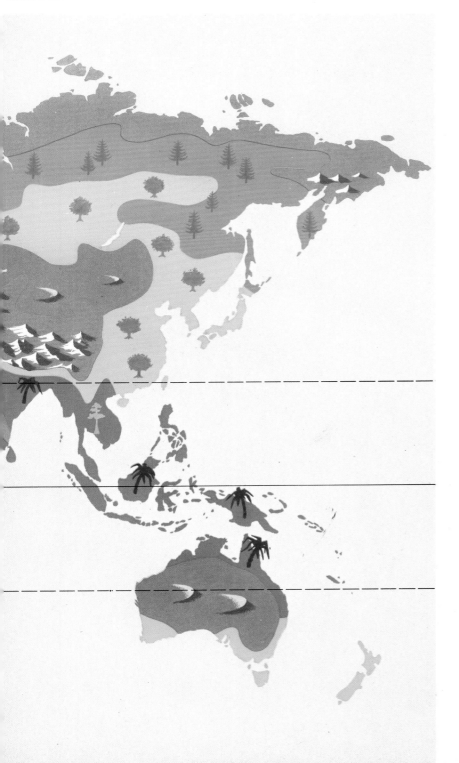

1

2

3

4

5

Peoples of the World

Samoyed Woman, Northern Russia

Mongolian Man

Japanese Woman

Turkish Man

Tibetan Herdsman on a Yak

Jewish Man, Israel

Afghanistan Man

Chinese Woman

Korean Man

Persian Man and Woman, Iran

Sheik, Arabia

Sikh Man, India

Hindu Woman, India

Vietnamese Woman

Burmese Woman

Dancing Girl, Thailand

Dyak Man, Borneo

Malay Man

Vedda Man, Sri Lanka

Batak Man Sumatra

Asia has more people than any other continent and surprisingly it has the greatest variety of peoples. Among them are the Mongols in the north, the Arabs and Turks in the west, the Indonesians in the south-east, and the Chinese and Japanese in the east. These different peoples wear many beautiful and varied traditional costumes.

Many different types of people are found throughout the world. They often vary as much between countries in the same continent as they do between different continents. The following pages show some of the world's people in their traditional dress. National costumes are still worn in some countries, but today, more and more people all over the world are wearing Western clothing.

Europeans vary between the tall, blond people of Scandinavia and the shorter dark-haired people near the Mediterranean. Nowadays these people are intermixed and the main differences are between their languages and their culture. It is becoming more and more rare to see them in their national costume except on special occasions, such as weddings and festivals.

Lapp Woman and Child, Finland

Norwegian Man

Swedish Girl

Cossack Man, Russia

Scotsman

Danish Girl

Welsh Girl

Dutch Girl, Netherlands

Hungarian Man

Polish Girl

Black Forest Girl, Germany

Tyrolean Man, Austria

Normandy Girl, France

Serbian Man, Yugoslavia

Spanish Man and Woman

Italian Woman

Greek Man

17

Canadian Eskimo
and Child

Alaskan Eskimo

Kutchin Man

Cheyenne
Warrior

Apache
Warrior

Iroquois
Woman

The Indians of America came across
the Bering Strait from Asia and spread all
over the vast American continent.
Although they are all descended from the
same Asian ancestors, the dress and
customs of the many tribes vary greatly.
The picture shows just some of the many
Indian tribes. Today, they make up only a
small part of America's huge population.

Sioux Chief

Navaho
Woman

Seminole
Woman

Mexican Man

Carib Woman,
Guyana

Ticuna Man,
Brazil

The people of Oceania wearing their
traditional dress are some of the people
that the European explorers found when
they came to Australia, New Zealand, and
the Pacific Islands. Most of the people in
Australia and New Zealand today are
descended from Europeans.

Tzotzil Woman,
Guatemala

Quillacinga Man,
Colombia

New Guinea
Tribesman

Yap Woman,
Caroline
Islands

Fijian
Girl

Aymara Man,
Peru

Quechua Woman,
Bolivia

Bororo Man,
Brazil

Australian
Aborigine

Maori Girl,
New Zealand

Araucarian
Woman, Chile

Tehuelche Man,
Patagonia

Ona Woman,
Tierra del Fuego

18

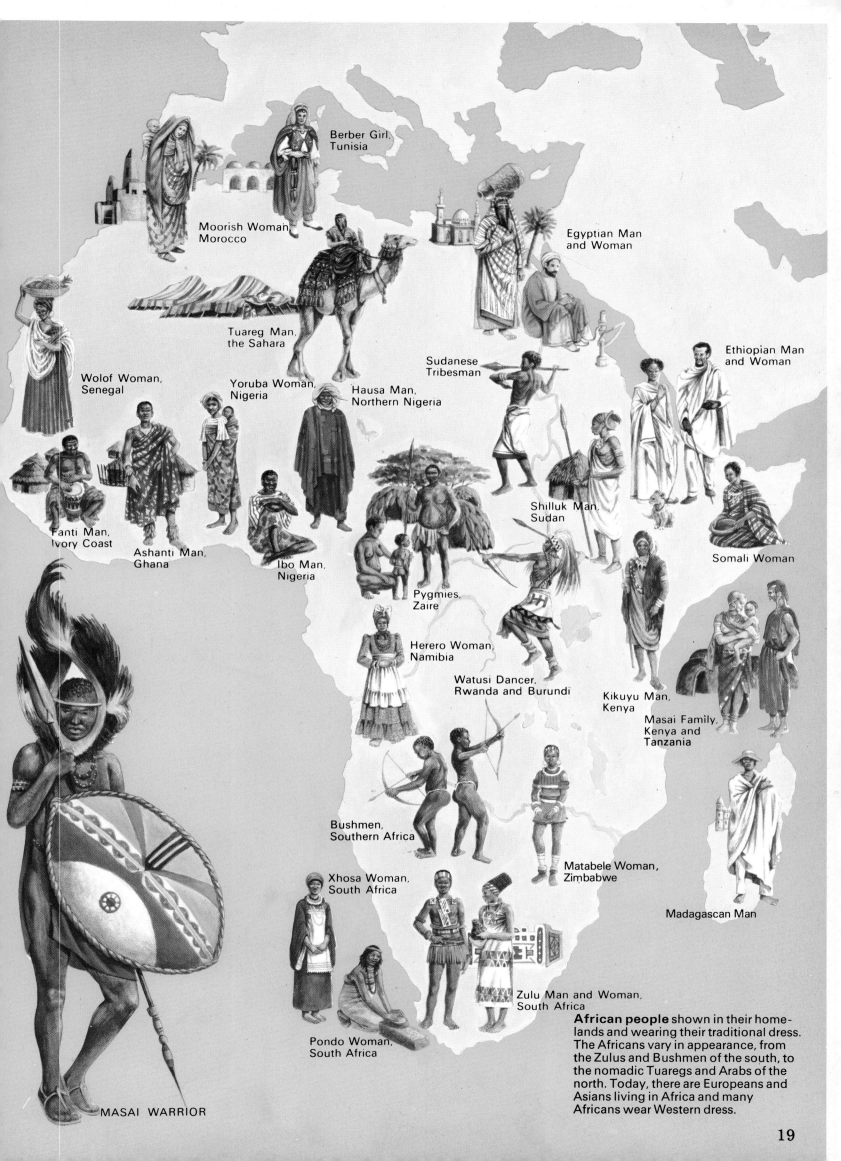

Berber Girl, Tunisia

Moorish Woman Morocco

Tuareg Man, the Sahara

Egyptian Man and Woman

Ethiopian Man and Woman

Sudanese Tribesman

Wolof Woman, Senegal

Yoruba Woman, Nigeria

Hausa Man, Northern Nigeria

Shilluk Man, Sudan

Somali Woman

Fanti Man, Ivory Coast

Ashanti Man, Ghana

Ibo Man, Nigeria

Pygmies, Zaire

Herero Woman, Namibia

Watusi Dancer, Rwanda and Burundi

Kikuyu Man, Kenya

Masai Family, Kenya and Tanzania

Bushmen, Southern Africa

Matabele Woman, Zimbabwe

Madagascan Man

Xhosa Woman, South Africa

Zulu Man and Woman, South Africa

Pondo Woman, South Africa

MASAI WARRIOR

African people shown in their home-lands and wearing their traditional dress. The Africans vary in appearance, from the Zulus and Bushmen of the south, to the nomadic Tuaregs and Arabs of the north. Today, there are Europeans and Asians living in Africa and many Africans wear Western dress.

Polar Lands

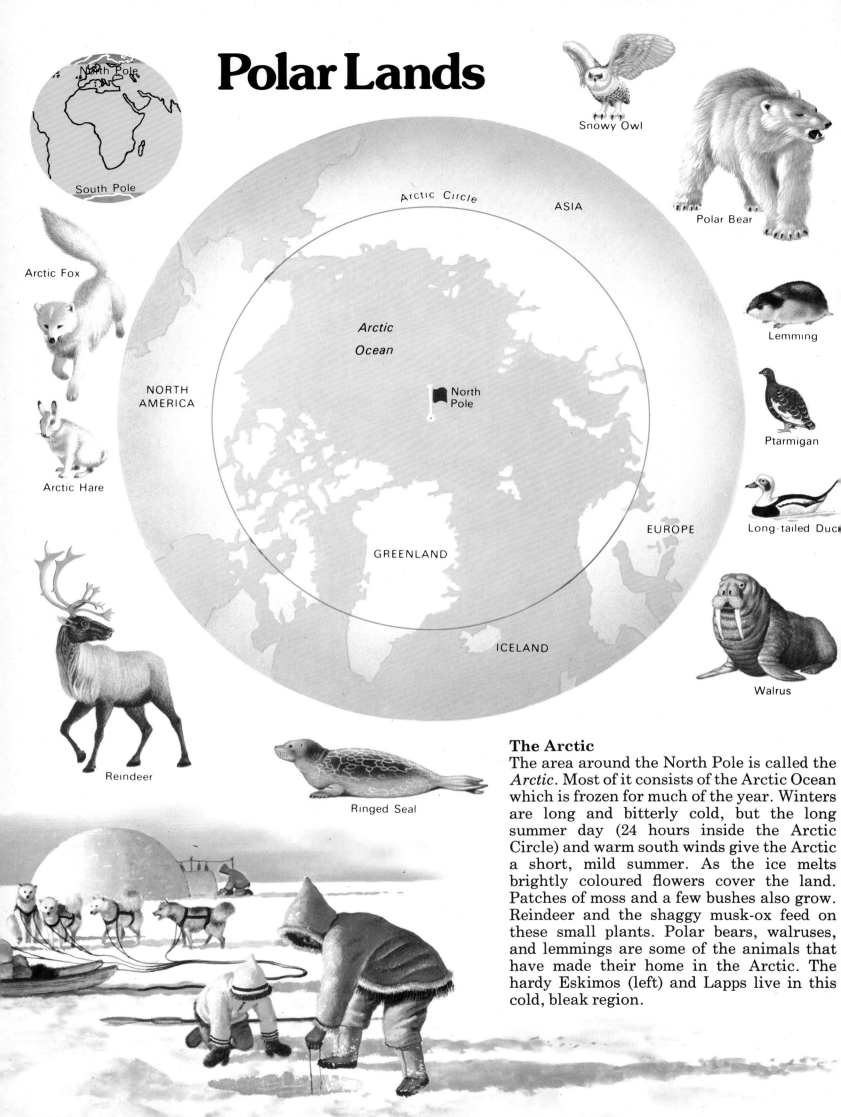

North Pole

South Pole

Snowy Owl

Polar Bear

Arctic Circle

ASIA

Arctic Fox

Lemming

NORTH
AMERICA

Arctic
Ocean

North
Pole

Ptarmigan

Arctic Hare

Long-tailed Duck

EUROPE

GREENLAND

Walrus

Reindeer

ICELAND

Ringed Seal

The Arctic

The area around the North Pole is called the *Arctic*. Most of it consists of the Arctic Ocean which is frozen for much of the year. Winters are long and bitterly cold, but the long summer day (24 hours inside the Arctic Circle) and warm south winds give the Arctic a short, mild summer. As the ice melts brightly coloured flowers cover the land. Patches of moss and a few bushes also grow. Reindeer and the shaggy musk-ox feed on these small plants. Polar bears, walruses, and lemmings are some of the animals that have made their home in the Arctic. The hardy Eskimos (left) and Lapps live in this cold, bleak region.

The Antarctic

The *Antarctic* is a vast ice-clad continent one and a half times as big as the United States. It is the coldest continent, with more than 90 per cent of the world's snow and ice. Plant life grows only near the coast where snow and ice melt in summer. Sea birds, including penguins, skuas, and snowy petrels are plentiful in the Antarctic. Some birds spend only summer in the Antarctic, flying north to warmer lands when the winter comes. The continent is so remote and the climate so severe that few people have settled there. A few people spend short periods at weather stations and research bases (see picture on the right).

Adélie Penguins

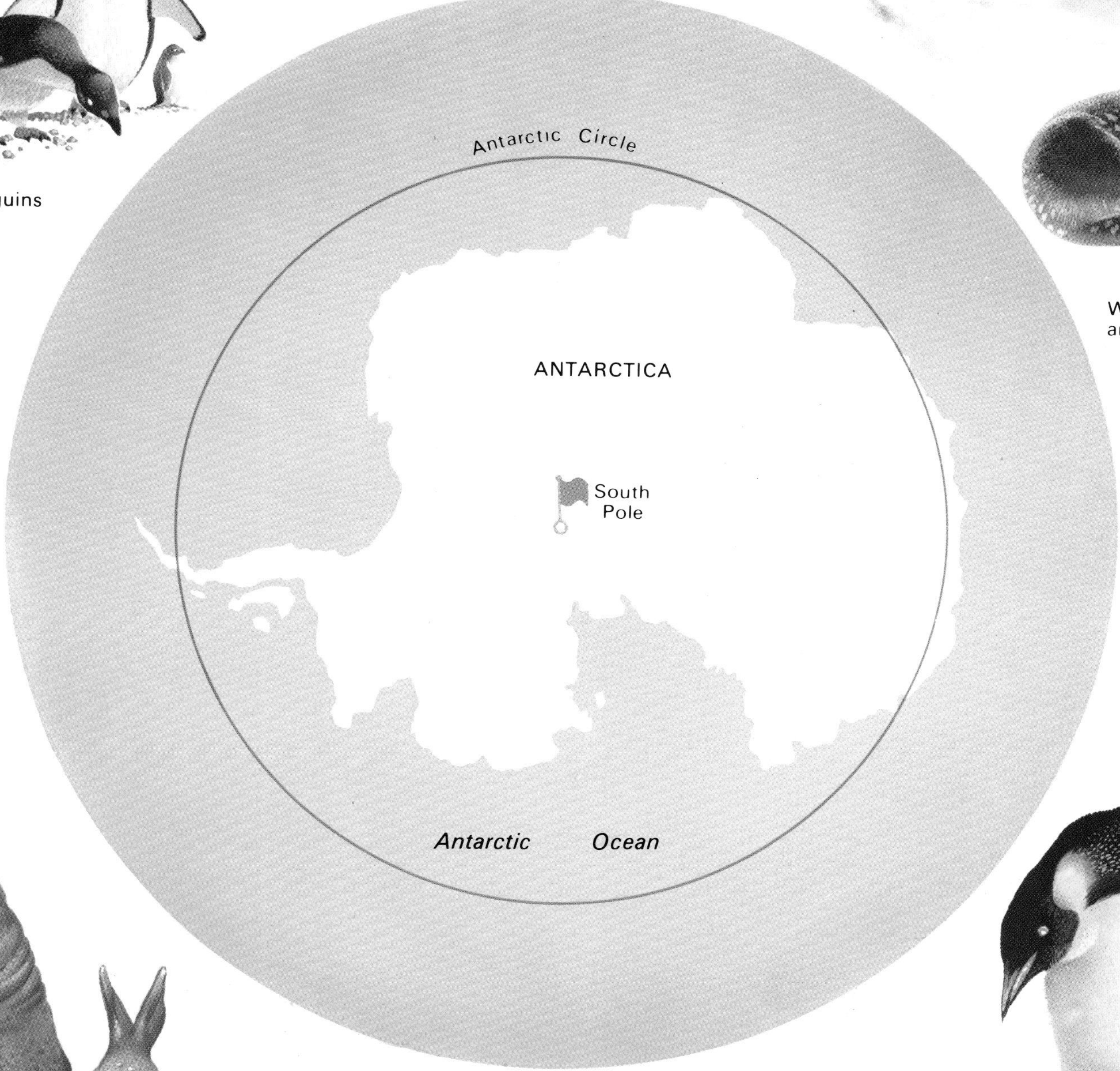

Weddell Seal and Young

Skua

Snowy Petrel

Antarctic Circle

ANTARCTICA

South Pole

Antarctic Ocean

Elephant Seal

Fulmar

Emperor Penguin and Chick

21

Europe

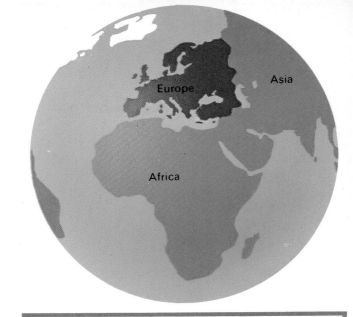

Europe covers only one-fifteenth of the land surface of the world. Despite its small size, it has had more influence on the rest of the world than any other continent. From ancient times up to the present Europe has played an important part in the development and progress of the world.

Europe stretches from the Arctic Ocean in the north to the Mediterranean Sea in the south, and from the Atlantic Ocean in the west to the rugged Ural Mountains in Russia in the east. Because Europe and Asia are not separated by water, some people think of them as one vast continent, which they call *Eurasia*.

Europe is full of contrasts—snow-covered mountains, lush green valleys, and sun-parched plains. It can be divided into four main areas. *The Central Plain* covers the biggest part of Europe, from France to European Russia. It has many of Europe's main cities. Its mild climate and fertile land has made this region very important for farming. *The North-West Highlands* are found in Scandinavia, north-western Russia, north-western France, Ireland, and north-western Great Britain. Here the climate is cool and wet. The steep mountain slopes and poor soils make it unsuitable for farming. *The Central Uplands* which run from Czechoslovakia to Portugal is an area of low mountains and plateaus, and vast forests. Many of Europe's largest coalfields are found here. *The Alpine Mountain System* crosses southern Europe. Several mountain ranges including the Alps and Pyrenees are found here. It is a region of snow-capped peaks, forested mountain slopes, and fertile valleys.

Rivers and Canals

The rivers and canals of Europe add to the beauty of the scenery, but they are most important for draining farmland and providing transport routes.

Europe's longest river is the Volga. It flows 3685 kilometres through Russia to the Caspian Sea. Other major rivers are the Don, the Rhine, and the Danube. Many barges, boats, and ships use these rivers to carry goods to different parts of Europe.

The rivers of Scandinavia are short and fast-flowing. They are not suitable for travelling on but they give power to make electricity.

Europe has many canals, particularly in The Netherlands, where they also help to drain the land. The biggest is the Kiel Canal in Germany which is a short route between the Baltic and the North Sea.

The Alps are a great mountain chain in southern Europe. They were once thought to be dangerous and people were frightened to cross them. But today the many passes and tunnels have made crossing them easy. They have become one of the most popular winter sports and mountaineering areas of the world.

ARCTIC
OCEAN

The tundra is an area of cold, frozen land where no trees can grow. It is the home of the Lapps and their herds of reindeer.

URAL MOUNTAINS

Forests cover many areas in northern Europe. Much of the world's timber is grown in the forests of Russia.

Scandinavian coasts have many fiords. They are steep-sided valleys filled with sea water. The valleys were originally carved out by glaciers.

SCANDINAVIAN MOUNTAINS

LAKE ONEGA

LAKE LADOGA

Volga

Rolling plains and a mild climate make much of Europe good for farming.

VANERN

BALTIC SEA

EUROPEAN PLAIN

Don

LANTIC CEAN

Ben Nevis ▲   Grampians

NORTH SEA

Pennines

Thames

The canals of Holland drain the land and are important for transport.

Kiel Canal

Elbe

NORTH

Vistula

The River Rhine winds its way over 1000 kilometres to the sea. It cuts through deep gorges lined with vineyards.

Dnieper

ENGLISH CHANNEL

Seine

Rhine

CARPATHIAN MTS

The flat lands of north and central France are suitable for growing crops and grazing cows.

Loire

Garonne

ALPS

Mt Blanc

Mt Dore

Rhône

Po

Danube

BLACK SEA

PYRENEES

ouro

us

Ebro

Apennines

Tiber

ADRIATIC SEA

Vesuvius

AEGEAN SEA

Etna

MEDITERRANEAN SEA

Mediterranean coasts have beautiful beaches and are popular holiday resorts.

The fertile lands around the Mediterranean Sea and the rivers of southern Europe are important for their vine growing.

The Greek islands are dotted in the Aegean Sea off the coast of south-east Europe. They are important for olive growing. Grapes are grown for wine, currants and sultanas.

23

Amsterdam (above), the capital of The Netherlands, is famous for its canals. The canals divide the city into many small islands which are connected by hundreds of bridges.

Moscow is the capital of Russia. Below is Red Square with St Basil's cathedral in the background.

Paris (below) has long been the centre of fashion and art in Europe. Its many parks and fine buildings make it one of the most beautiful cities in the world. The picture shows artists' stalls in front of Paris' most famous church, the Notre Dame.

People and Countries of Europe

The people of Europe are made up of many different nationalities. They each have their own customs, traditions and language. More than 40 different languages are spoken, as well as many dialects (local languages). Such is the variety of peoples in Europe that more than one language is often spoken in a single country. In Belgium some people speak French, others Flemish; in Great Britain the Welsh have a separate language of their own; and in Switzerland French, German, and Italian are spoken.

Over 650 million people live in Europe. Even though it is the second smallest of the continents it is more densely populated (it has more people in a square kilometre) than any other continent. Most of the people live in large cities. These heavily populated areas form a broad belt stretching from London, through Paris, Brussels, Hamburg and Berlin, to the Ukraine region in Russia (the USSR). However, there are some parts of Europe, particularly in the far north, with wide open spaces and no people living there.

There are 35 countries in Europe. They vary enormously in size, from the Vatican City (the world's smallest country) to Europe's largest country—the part of Russia that lies in Europe. (The rest of Russia covers the entire northern part of the Asian continent.)

Today, the countries of Europe are divided by a political barrier called the *Iron Curtain*. This separates Western Europe from Eastern (Communist) Europe. However, many nations on both sides of the Iron Curtain are working more closely together. Several nations of Western Europe have formed the European Economic Community (the *Common Market*). Some people think that one day there might be a United States of Europe.

Christianity is the major religion in Europe and most European Christians are Roman Catholics. The centre of the Roman Catholic religion is the Vatican City. The picture on the right shows the Pope in St Peter's, the largest Christian church in the world.

London (below), is the capital of the United Kingdom and the largest city in Europe.

ICELAND
■ Reykjavik

SWEDEN

NORWAY
Bergen •
• Oslo ■
Stockholm ■

FINLAND
Helsinki ■   • Leningrad

■ Moscow

**RUSSIA
(USSR)**

**REPUBLIC
OF
IRELAND
(Eire)**

**UNITED
KINGDOM**
Edinburgh •
Glasgow •
• Belfast
Dublin ■   Liverpool •
Manchester •
Cardiff •   Birmingham •
London ■

DENMARK
Copenhagen ■   • Malmo

POLAND
Warsaw ■

Hamburg •
**WEST
GERMANY**
**THE
NETHER-
LANDS**   Amsterdam •
Rotterdam •
Brussels •
BELGIUM
Luxembourg
1
• Paris
Bonn ■
Frankfurt •

East
Berlin ■
**EAST
GERMANY**
Prague ■
CZECHOSLOVAKIA

FRANCE
• Nantes

Munich •
Bern •
SWITZERLAND
Geneva •
• Lyon
• Milan
• Turin

Vienna ■
AUSTRIA
HUNGARY
Budapest ■

ROMANIA
Bucharest ■

Bordeaux •

• Venice

Belgrade ■
YUGOSLAVIA
BULGARIA
• Sofia ■

Istanbul •

MONACO
• Marseilles

ANDORRA

**VATICAN
CITY**
• Rome
**SAN
MARINO**

Tirana ■
ALBANIA

• Barcelona
ITALY
Naples •

Corsica

GREECE
■ Athens

Lisbon

■ Madrid
• Valencia

Sardinia

Balearic Is.

SPAIN

Palermo •

Sicily

Crete

GIBRALTAR

Valletta ■
MALTA

EUROPE
■ Capital Cities
• Other Cities

1. Luxembourg
2. Liechtenstein

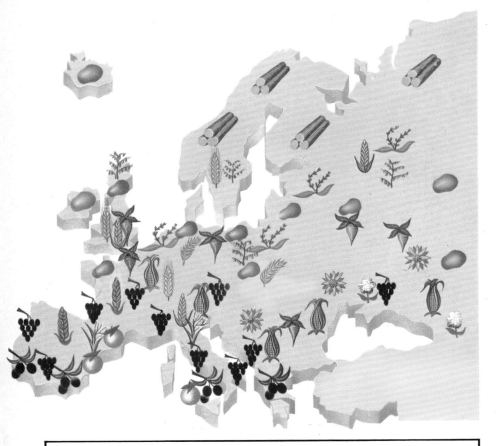

The Wealth of Europe

Europe has some of the world's richest farmland. Almost one-third of the people of Europe work on farms. Dairy farming and cattle breeding can be found in most parts of the continent—Denmark, The Netherlands, and Great Britain, for instance, are famous for their butter and cheese.

Europe's main crops are wheat, oats, and barley, but a lot of sugar beet and potatoes are also grown in many areas. Around the Mediterranean, olives, oranges, and other fruits are grown in large quantities. In southern Europe large vineyards grow in the valleys and on the mountain slopes. France, in particular, is world famous for the variety of its fine wines.

In the far north the soil and climate are poor and so the farms are small. Here, the main wealth comes from the vast forests which give a valuable supply of timber.

CROPS

Timber	Barley	Rye
Sunflowers	Oats	Flax
Olives	Sugar Beet	Potatoes
Cotton	Citrus Fruit	Grapes
Wheat	Maize	Rice

Mixed farms are those with both crops and livestock. In Europe mixed farming is common, but it varies from region to region. In the north rye, oats, barley, and cattle are important. In central Europe the main crops are wheat and sugar beet; the livestock are dairy and beef cattle, pigs, and sometimes sheep.

Vines (right) are grown throughout the warm Mediterranean countries and in parts of central Europe, particularly France and Germany. Europe is world famous for its fine wines.

Europe's very long coastline (over 80,000 kilometres), indented with lots of rivers and other inlets, has meant that many areas depend on fishing. The natural harbours provided by the uneven coastline have helped many European countries develop important fishing and shipping industries.

Most of Europe's industry is found in East Germany, France, Great Britain, Italy, Russia, and West Germany—six of the world's ten top manufacturing countries. The most famous of these industrial centres is the Ruhr in West Germany. Other major centres are the Midlands in Great Britain, and the Urals and Donbass in Russia.

Industry has largely developed because Europe has a huge mineral wealth. Iron ore, zinc, tin, lead, copper, and coal are found in some areas. Recently large amounts of oil and natural gas have been found in the North Sea. Such is Europe's rich variety of minerals that even platinum, silver, and gold are mined in some parts.

The Ruhr is the main industrial centre of West Germany. The factories were built here because of the rich coalfields in this region.

Timber from the great forests of Scandinavia is floated down rivers to sawmills (left) where it is cut into boards.

The Fiat car factory (below left) outside Turin in Italy. Fiat is Europe's second biggest car manufacturer.

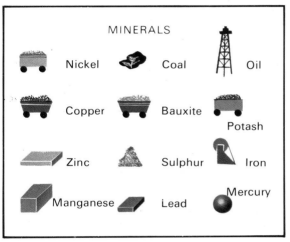

MINERALS

Nickel	Coal	Oil
Copper	Bauxite	Potash
Zinc	Sulphur	Iron
Manganese	Lead	Mercury

Razorbill*

Reindeer

Elk

Wolverine

Capercaillie*

Great
Black-backed Gull*

Wildcat*

Robin*

White
Stork*

Wild

Hedgehog*

Otter*

Grey Heron*

Red Deer*

Rabbit*

Badger*

Fallow Deer*

Great Spotted
Woodpecker*

Common
Toad*

Red Squirrel*

Golden Eagle

Barn Owl*

Marmot

Chamois

Pyrenean Ibex

Green
Lizard

Land Tortoise

Lynx

Adder*

Mouflon

Crested Porcupine

Animals marked with an asterik (*) are found
in many parts of the continent.

Bezoar
Goat

Wolf

Brown Bear

Roe Deer

Stoat*

Hare*

European Wildlife

Europe was once almost completely covered in forest. Today a lot of the forest has been cleared to make way for cities, roads, and farms. Some animals, such as red foxes and weasels have learned to live in these new surroundings. But others, such as the European bison and the wild horse, have vanished from the countryside.

While some animals have disappeared altogether, others are in danger of dying out. Even the common otter, which is found in most parts of the continent, is becoming rare. The Spanish lynx was once common but now only a few survive in the very south of Spain. But, it is surprising how many animals have managed to survive the destruction of their natural surroundings. Efforts are now being made to ensure that they, too, are not forced from their homes.

Animals of the northern forests include elk, brown bears, chipmunks, and capercaillies. Many birds spend summer in the north but winter in the warmer lands farther south. Among the great variety of birds in Europe are large species such as eagles, storks, and owls as well as many smaller kinds. Reindeer live in the colder lands to the north of the forests.

Other types of deer, polecats, boar, and wildcats are common in the pockets of woodland and moorland farther south. Squirrels, foxes, badgers, rabbits, and hedgehogs are among the animals that are widespread all over Europe.

The wood mouse lives on the woodland floors, eating mainly berries, buds, and seeds. It also gathers nuts which it stores near its nest. The wood mouse cracks open nuts with its very sharp teeth.

The purple emperor butterfly is another European woodland creature. It flits around the tops of oak trees and feeds on oak leaves.

The red fox is found all over Europe. It eats mice and voles, but is sometimes found rummaging around dustbins and rubbish dumps.

Asia

Asia, the largest continent, has an area of 44 million square kilometres and covers one-third of the Earth's land surface. It extends from the frozen Arctic in the north to the hot, wet tropics in the south.

Asia is a continent of opposites. It has both the highest and the lowest land points on the Earth. Mount Everest on the border between Nepal and Tibet is the highest, soaring to 8848 metres. The Dead Sea shore between Israel and Jordan is the lowest, at 397 metres below sea level.

Asia has rain-drenched jungles and parched deserts, and its climate includes some of the hottest and coldest parts of the world. In some areas densely populated cities sprawl over the land while in others there are vast barren wastes in which no-one lives.

In the south-west are the countries of the Middle East. The greater part of these are either dry deserts or mountains. The centre of the continent is a wild, mountainous region. North-east of these mountains is the Gobi Desert, home of the wandering Mongol people. Farther north are broad lowlands and low plateaus that stretch to the Arctic Ocean. Little grows here because the land is completely frozen for much of the year. South of the central mountains the climate is completely different. Winds called *monsoons* blow regularly, often bringing heavy rains. Because of the plentiful water and fertile soils the best farming lands of Asia are found in the river valleys of the south and east.

The Roof of the World

Asia has many great mountain ranges. The largest, the Himalayas, stretches for 4000 kilometres and includes over 100 peaks above 7000 metres. Mount Everest, the highest of all, is among them. This area of lofty peaks is sometimes called *The Roof of the World.*

Desert covers much of south-west Asia (the Middle East). In these dry lands are found some of the world's largest oil fields.

The rivers of Asia play an important part in the lives of the people. The fertile valleys are ideal for growing crops (in the picture rice is being planted in terraced fields). The villages and towns are mostly in the valleys. Rivers are also used for carrying goods and people.

Important rivers are the Ganges, Indus, Brahmaputra, Mekong, Irrawaddy, Hwang-Ho, Si-Kiang, and Yangtse-Kiang—probably the busiest river in the world.

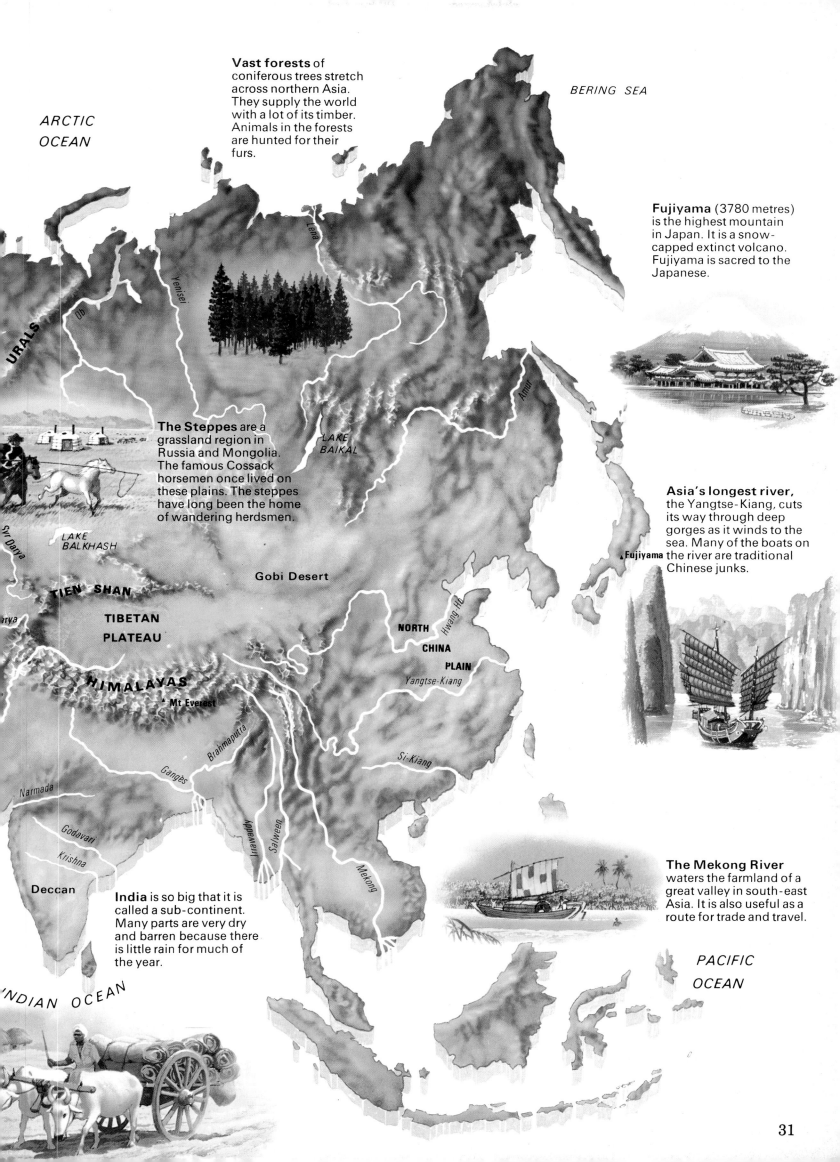

ARCTIC
OCEAN

BERING SEA

Vast forests of coniferous trees stretch across northern Asia. They supply the world with a lot of its timber. Animals in the forests are hunted for their furs.

Fujiyama (3780 metres) is the highest mountain in Japan. It is a snow-capped extinct volcano. Fujiyama is sacred to the Japanese.

URALS

Ob

Yenisei

Lena

Amur

The Steppes are a grassland region in Russia and Mongolia. The famous Cossack horsemen once lived on these plains. The steppes have long been the home of wandering herdsmen.

LAKE BAIKAL

Syr Darya

LAKE BALKHASH

Asia's longest river, the Yangtse-Kiang, cuts its way through deep gorges as it winds to the sea. Many of the boats on the river are traditional Chinese junks.

▲Fujiyama

TIEN SHAN

TIBETAN PLATEAU

Gobi Desert

arya

NORTH
CHINA
PLAIN

Hwang Ho

HIMALAYAS

▲ Mt Everest

Yangtse-Kiang

Brahmaputra

Ganges

Si-Kiang

Narmada

Godavari

Krishna

Irrawaddy

Salween

Mekong

Deccan

India is so big that it is called a sub-continent. Many parts are very dry and barren because there is little rain for much of the year.

The Mekong River waters the farmland of a great valley in south-east Asia. It is also useful as a route for trade and travel.

PACIFIC
OCEAN

INDIAN OCEAN

People and Countries of Asia

Asia, with a population of over 2000 million, is the home of over half the people in the world. Yet huge areas in the continent are so wild and barren that no-one can live there. People have crowded along river valleys and around the coasts of the south and east where they can farm. A third of the world's people live in just two countries—China, with the largest population in the world, and India, with the second largest. They have become so overcrowded, particularly in the large cities, that food is scarce.

A great many different kinds of people live in Asia. Most of them are *Mongoloids*. These include the Chinese, Japanese, Koreans, Siberians, and Mongols. Others include Indians, Arabs, Iranians, Turks, and Jews. They are all very different in their traditions, languages, religions, and ways of life.

Asia is sometimes called *the cradle of human culture*. In ancient times it was the centre for the world's earliest civilizations. All the greatest religions began in Asia. From the south-west came Judaism, Christianity, and Islam; from the south, Hinduism and Buddhism; and from the east, Confucianism, Taoism, and Shintoism.

Asians were the first farmers and traders. They also built the first cities, set up the first law systems, and invented paper and writing. The art and culture of Asia is still much admired by people in the West.

A Japanese family wearing traditional dress enjoys a meal.
Rice is the basic food of most Japanese. Food is usually served in small bowls and eaten with chopsticks.

Hinduism is the oldest living religion in the world. Hindu people bathe in the river Ganges in India (left). They believe that the river is sacred.

Hong Kong harbour is crowded with floating homes (below).
Thousands of people live in them because there is not enough space on the land.

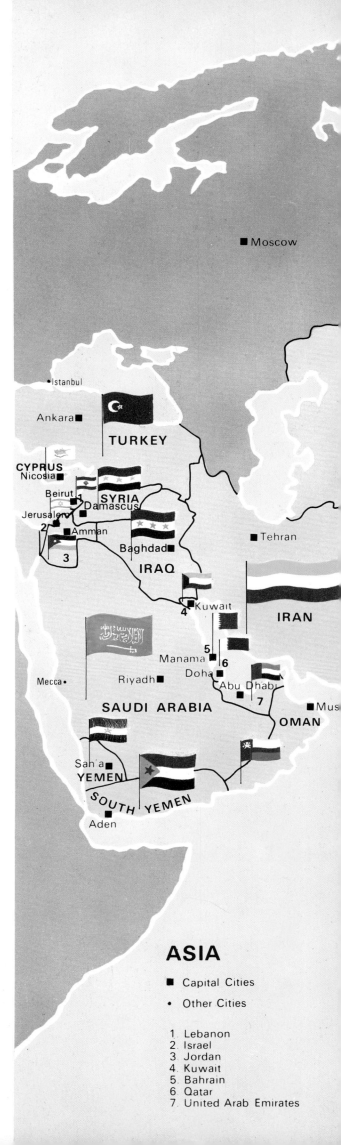

ASIA

■ Capital Cities

• Other Cities

1. Lebanon
2. Israel
3. Jordan
4. Kuwait
5. Bahrain
6. Qatar
7. United Arab Emirates

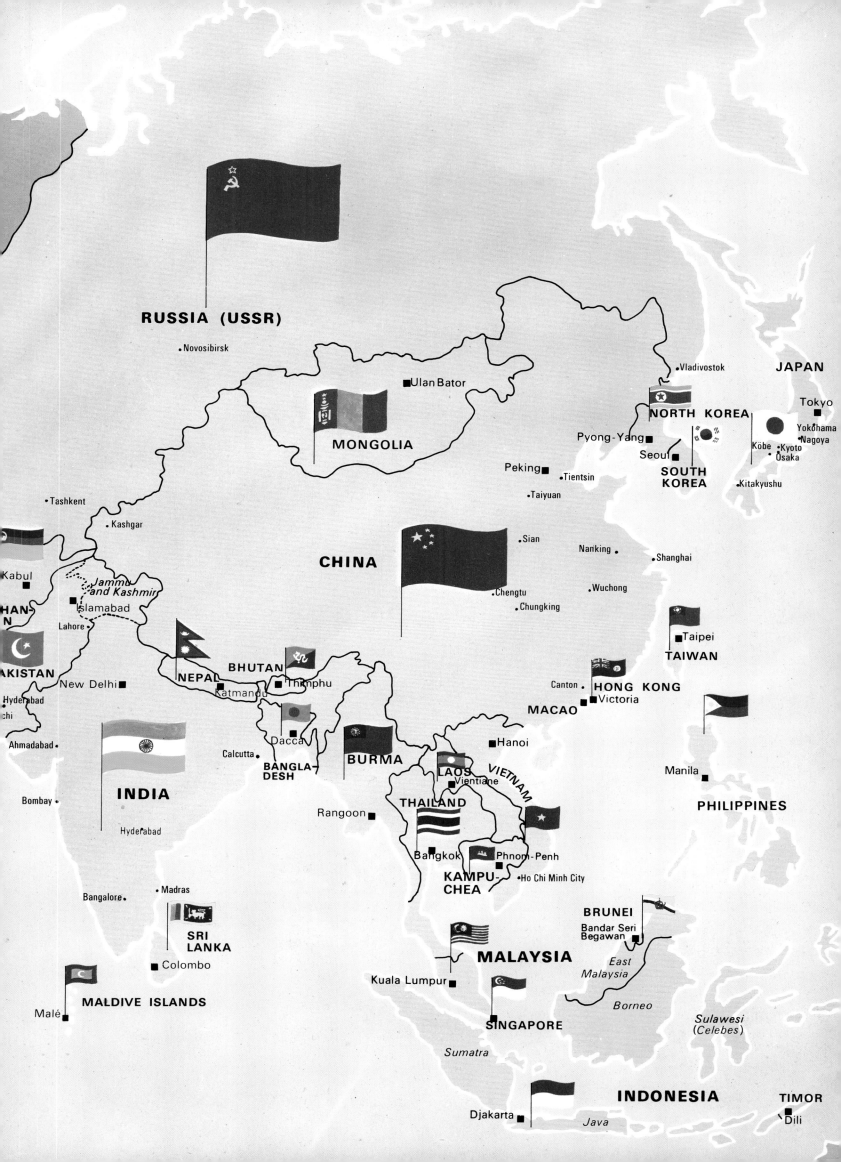

RUSSIA (USSR)

•Novosibirsk

•Vladivostok

JAPAN

■Ulan Bator

MONGOLIA

NORTH KOREA

Tokyo•

Pyong-Yang■

Yokohama
Nagoya

Seoul■

Kōbe• •Kyoto
•Osaka

**SOUTH
KOREA**

•Kitakyushu

•Tashkent

Peking■ •Tientsin

•Kashgar

•Taiyuan

Kabul■

•Sian

Nanking• •Shanghai

CHINA

**HAN
N**

Jammu
and Kashmir

Islamabad■

•Chengtu

•Wuchong

•Chungking

Lahore•

TAIWAN

•Taipei

PAKISTAN

NEPAL

BHUTAN

New Delhi•

Katmandu

•Thimphu

Canton• **HONG KONG**

MACAO

•Victoria

Hyderabad■

•Ahmadabad

Dacca■

Calcutta•

BURMA

•Hanoi

**BANGLA-
DESH**

LAOS

VIETNAM

Manila•

INDIA

Vientiane•

THAILAND

PHILIPPINES

Bombay•

Rangoon■

Hyderabad•

Bangkok•

Phnom-Penh•

•Ho Chi Minh City

Bangalore•

•Madras

**KAMPU-
CHEA**

BRUNEI

**SRI
LANKA**

Bandar Seri
Begawan

■Colombo

MALAYSIA

*East
Malaysia*

MALDIVE ISLANDS

Kuala Lumpur■

Borneo

Malé■

*Sulawesi
(Celebes)*

SINGAPORE

Sumatra

INDONESIA

TIMOR

Djakarta■

Java

•Dili

The Wealth of Asia

Farmers in southern Asia rely on heavy monsoon rains and ice melting in the mountains to flood their rivers, and so water their land. The wet land is suitable for growing rice which is the main food for millions of Asians.

In the drier areas crops such as maize, soybeans, and groundnuts grow well. India and Russia are also great wheat producing countries and tea, cotton, and sugarcane have been cultivated in Asia for centuries.

The dense forests of Burma give us a lot of timber, particularly teak. Timber, mainly pine, is also an important product of the northern forests of Russia. Most of the

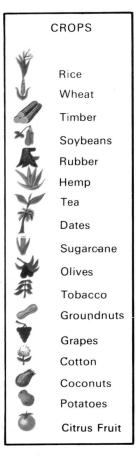

Oxen help to pull this farmer's plough in India.

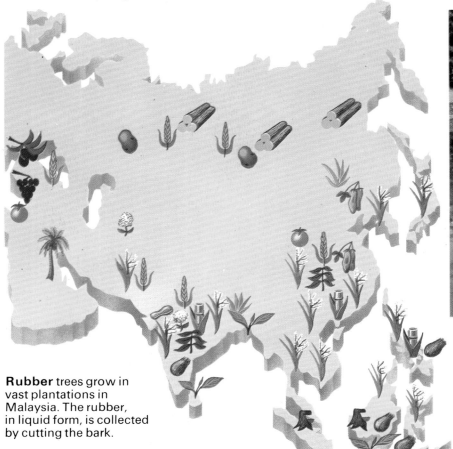

CROPS

Rice
Wheat
Timber
Soybeans
Rubber
Hemp
Tea
Dates
Sugarcane
Olives
Tobacco
Groundnuts
Grapes
Cotton
Coconuts
Potatoes
Citrus Fruit

Rubber trees grow in vast plantations in Malaysia. The rubber, in liquid form, is collected by cutting the bark.

Rice is the main diet for most Asians. These people are planting rice in flooded fields called *paddy fields.*

Tea being picked on a plantation in Sri Lanka. Sri Lanka produces a third of the world's tea. Even though the name of the country was changed the name 'Ceylon tea' remains.

world's rubber comes from the forests of Malaysia and Indonesia.

Asia is rich in minerals which include gold, silver, diamonds, rubies, and emeralds. An important export is oil, from south-west and south-east Asia. South-east Asia also supplies the world with two-thirds of its tin. Big coalfields are found, for example, in Russia.

Industry is not very highly developed in much of Asia. Most of the heavy manufacturing takes place in Japan, Russia, China, and Israel. Among the things made there are cars, motorbikes, radios, cameras, and farm machinery. Japan is an important shipbuilding country. The rest of Asia still largely depends on farming. The only industry consists of local crafts. But Asia is gradually becoming more industrialized.

Electronic calculators are made in this Japanese factory. In recent years Japan has become one of the world's leading industrial nations.

MINERALS

Gold

Lead

Oil

Bauxite

Coal

Nickel

Tin

Copper

Iron

Tungsten

Manganese

Chromium

Silk threads are twisted into skeins in a silk factory in China. The art of making silk thread and cloth was known in China over 4000 years ago.

Tin being dredged from a river in Malaysia, the world's greatest producer of this metal.

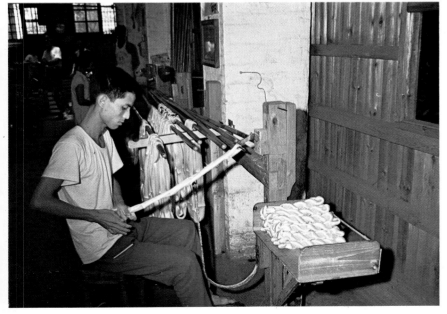

Asian Wildlife

Asia has an enormous variety of wildlife. Nearly every species of animal and plant can be found on the continent. There are also many animals and plants that live nowhere else in the world.

In the frozen north, reindeer are to be seen feeding on the mosses and lichens that grow there. It is the home of several Arctic birds, although many of them fly south in the cold winter months. Bears, foxes, and other furry animals roam the great forests farther south. Herds of horses, antelopes, camels, and sheep graze on the grassy, treeless plains of central Asia.

Asia has several species of tiger, including the biggest member of the cat family, the Siberian tiger. It lives in the mountains of Russia and Mongolia. Other tigers prowl in the tropical forests of southern Asia.

But it is in the southern part of the continent that the greatest variety of animals is to be found. There are apes, monkeys, leopards, rhinoceroses, and many colourful tropical birds. The south is also the home of many types of snake, including the regal cobra that, when threatened, spreads its frightening hood to ward off enemies.

Other animals have been tamed to help people with their work. In Burma, India, and Sri Lanka it is a common sight to see elephants moving heavy objects such as tree trunks. The Asian elephant is much smaller than the African elephant and its ears are only one-third the size of those of its African cousin.

Unfortunately, several Asian animals are threatened with extinction. These include furry creatures such as the sable, ermine, and marten. They have been ruthlessly hunted for their fur for hundreds of years, so now only a few remain. The orang-utan, the great ape found in Borneo is also in danger of dying out. Its name comes from the Malay language and means *old man of the woods*. Its natural home is rapidly disappearing because many of the forests in which it lives are being cleared for farms, factories and roads.

Tigers are found in the wild only in Asia. There are many different kinds of this strong and fierce and very cunning animal. This Bengali tiger roams the grasslands and jungles of India. During the heat of the day it often lies in the long grass, or even in swamps or shallow water.

The giant panda, found in the wild only in Asia, lives in the bamboo forests of west China.

Griffon Vulture

Caracal

Arabian Camel

Wild

Arabian Oryx

Brown Bear

Nuthatch

Reindeer

Saiga Antelope

Cormorant

Bactrian Camel

Flying Squirrel

Sika Deer

Yak

Golden Pheasant

Giant Panda

Elephant

Water Deer

Rhinoceros

Cobra

Tiger

Pangolin

Mandarin Duck

Hornbill

Rhesus Monkey

Monkey-eating Eagle

Blackbuck

Gaur

Tapir

Gibbon

Orang-utan

Civet

Flying Lizard

Tarsier

Peacock

Africa

Africa is a vast continent of grasslands, forests, and deserts. It covers an area of 30 million square kilometres and makes up one-fifth of the land area of the Earth. Africa stretches for over 8000 kilometres from north to south, and for over 7400 kilometres from east to west, so it is nearly as wide as it is long.

The whole of Africa consists of the world's largest plateau. The edges of this great tableland rise steeply at an average distance of 30 kilometres inland from the coast. It is higher in the east and south than it is in the west and north. The tableland is surrounded by a narrow coastal plain which makes up only a very small part of the total land area. Unlike Asia, Europe, and the Americas, Africa has no lofty mountain ranges.

Africa's two highest mountains, Mount Kilimanjaro and Mount Kenya, rise from the eastern part of the plateau. Nearby is Africa's largest lake, Lake Victoria. Lake Tanganyika, Lake Malawi, and a few other long, narrow lakes lie in a deep valley which runs more than 4800 kilometres from Syria, along the Red Sea, through Ethiopia, Kenya, and Malawi. It is called the *Great Rift Valley*. Rift valleys are formed when the land sinks between two breaks in the Earth's crust.

The equator runs almost through the middle of Africa. This region has a very hot, wet climate, and dense tropical forests. To the north and south of equatorial Africa stretch grassy plains called *savannas*. Beyond the savannas there are sun-parched deserts, the huge Sahara in the north and the Kalahari in the south. In the lands bordering the Mediterranean Sea in the far north, summers are long and hot and winters are mild. A similar climate is found around the Cape of Good Hope in the south. To the south-east of the continent is a large island called Madagascar, the fourth largest island in the world.

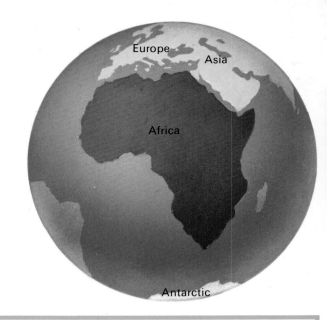

Rivers of Africa

Most of Africa's rivers have waterfalls and rapids. They are therefore very difficult for travelling on. Nevertheless they were an important means of travel for the early explorers. The ridge of mountains along the east coast of Africa makes the rivers on that side of the continent fairly short. Exceptions are the Zambezi (2576 km) and the Limpopo (1288 km) which flow to the Indian Ocean through gaps in the mountains. Africa's longest river, the Nile (6679 km), is also the longest in the world.

Victoria Falls

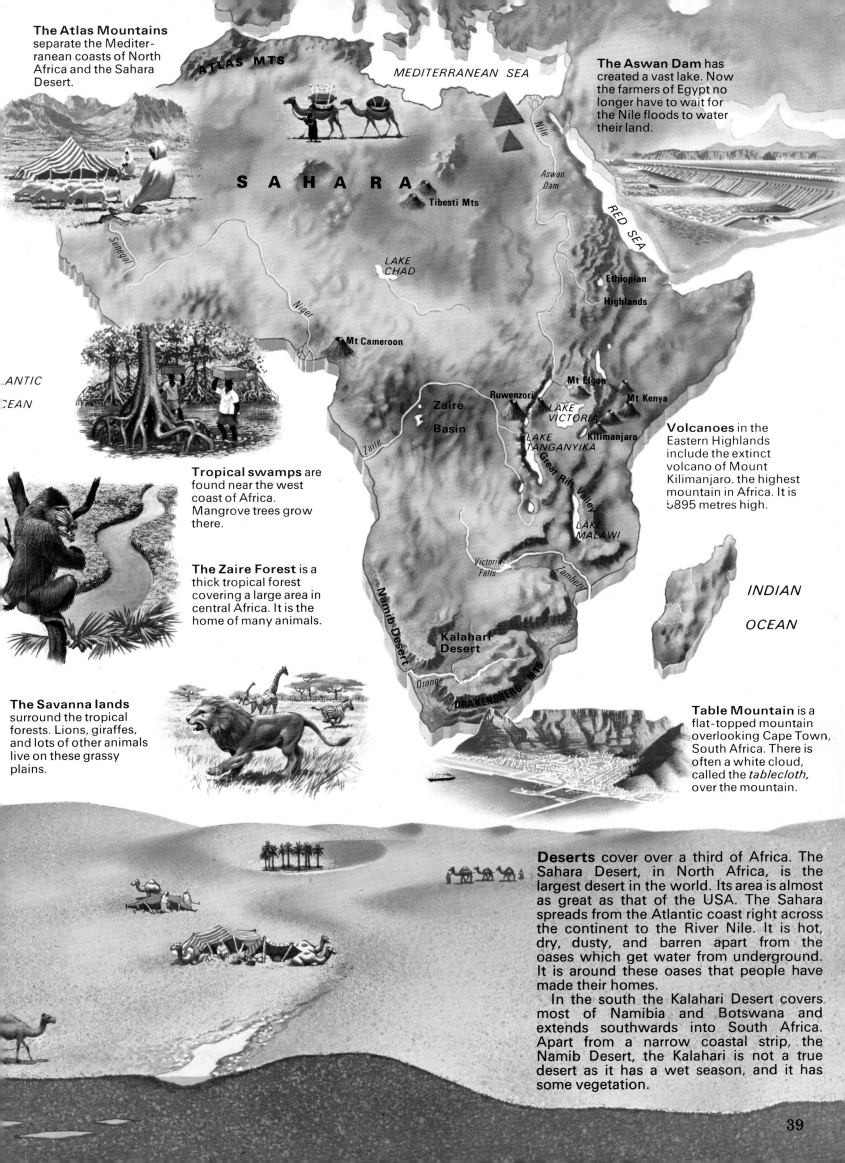

The Atlas Mountains separate the Mediterranean coasts of North Africa and the Sahara Desert.

ATLAS MTS

MEDITERRANEAN SEA

The Aswan Dam has created a vast lake. Now the farmers of Egypt no longer have to wait for the Nile floods to water their land.

S A H A R A

Tibesti Mts

Nile

Aswan Dam

RED SEA

Senegal

LAKE CHAD

Niger

Ethiopian Highlands

Mt Cameroon

ATLANTIC OCEAN

Zaire Basin

Zaire

Mt Elgon

Ruwenzori

LAKE VICTORIA

Mt Kenya

Kilimanjaro

LAKE TANGANYIKA

Great Rift Valley

LAKE MALAWI

Tropical swamps are found near the west coast of Africa. Mangrove trees grow there.

The Zaire Forest is a thick tropical forest covering a large area in central Africa. It is the home of many animals.

Volcanoes in the Eastern Highlands include the extinct volcano of Mount Kilimanjaro, the highest mountain in Africa. It is 5895 metres high.

Namib Desert

Victoria Falls

Zambezi

INDIAN OCEAN

Kalahari Desert

Orange

DRAKENSBERG MTS

The Savanna lands surround the tropical forests. Lions, giraffes, and lots of other animals live on these grassy plains.

Table Mountain is a flat-topped mountain overlooking Cape Town, South Africa. There is often a white cloud, called the *tablecloth*, over the mountain.

Deserts cover over a third of Africa. The Sahara Desert, in North Africa, is the largest desert in the world. Its area is almost as great as that of the USA. The Sahara spreads from the Atlantic coast right across the continent to the River Nile. It is hot, dry, dusty, and barren apart from the oases which get water from underground. It is around these oases that people have made their homes.

In the south the Kalahari Desert covers most of Namibia and Botswana and extends southwards into South Africa. Apart from a narrow coastal strip, the Namib Desert, the Kalahari is not a true desert as it has a wet season, and it has some vegetation.

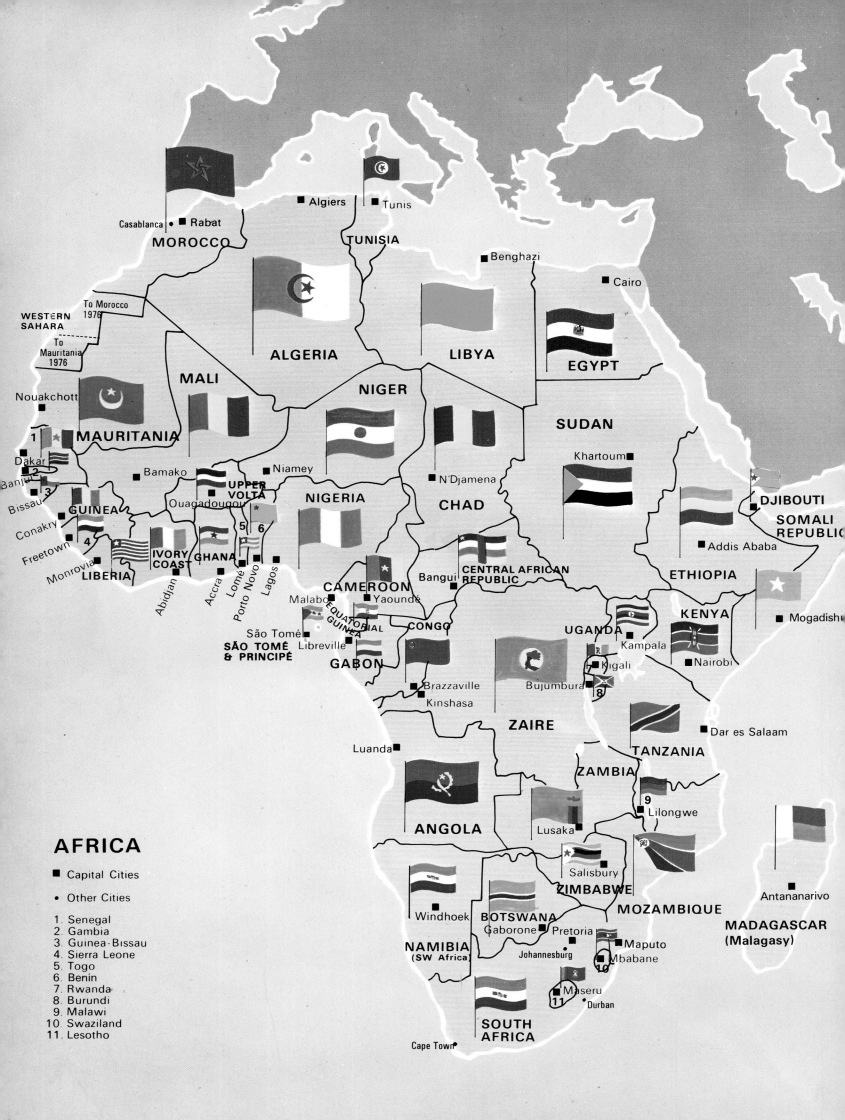

Casablanca • ■ Rabat
■ Algiers   ■ Tunis
■ Benghazi
■ Cairo

MOROCCO
TUNISIA

WESTERN
SAHARA
To Morocco
1976
To
Mauritania
1976

ALGERIA
LIBYA
EGYPT

MALI
NIGER
SUDAN

Nouakchott ■
MAURITANIA
■ Bamako
Niamey ■
Khartoum ■

1
Dakar ■
2
Banjul
3
Bissau
GUINEA
Conakry
4
Freetown
Monrovia
LIBERIA

UPPER
VOLTA
Ouagadougou
IVORY
COAST
GHANA
5 6
NIGERIA
N'Djamena ■
CHAD

Abidjan
Accra
Lomé
Porto Novo
Lagos
Malabo ■
EQUATORIAL
GUINEA
São Tomé ■
SÃO TOMÉ
& PRINCIPE
Libreville ■
GABON

CAMEROON
Yaoundé ■
Bangui ■
CENTRAL AFRICAN
REPUBLIC

CONGO
Brazzaville ■
Kinshasa ■

ZAIRE

Addis Ababa ■
ETHIOPIA

DJIBOUTI
SOMALI
REPUBLIC

Mogadishu ■

KENYA
UGANDA
Kampala ■
Nairobi ■
R
Kigali
7
8
Bujumbura ■

Dar es Salaam ■
TANZANIA

Luanda ■

ANGOLA

ZAMBIA
Lusaka ■
Lilongwe ■
9

AFRICA

■ Capital Cities

• Other Cities

1. Senegal
2. Gambia
3. Guinea-Bissau
4. Sierra Leone
5. Togo
6. Benin
7. Rwanda
8. Burundi
9. Malawi
10. Swaziland
11. Lesotho

Windhoek ■
NAMIBIA
(SW Africa)

BOTSWANA
Gaborone ■

Salisbury ■
ZIMBABWE

MOZAMBIQUE

Antananarivo ■
MADAGASCAR
(Malagasy)

Pretoria ■
Johannesburg •
Maputo ■
Mbabane
10
Maseru ■
11
Durban •

SOUTH
AFRICA

Cape Town •

40

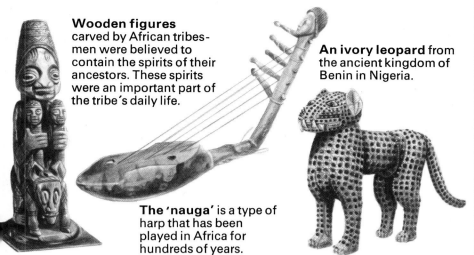

Wooden figures carved by African tribesmen were believed to contain the spirits of their ancestors. These spirits were an important part of the tribe's daily life.

An ivory leopard from the ancient kingdom of Benin in Nigeria.

The 'nauga' is a type of harp that has been played in Africa for hundreds of years.

People and Countries of Africa

Africa was once known as the *Dark Continent* because so little was known about it. Only in the 19th century was inland Africa explored. Before that people came only to the coastal areas to trade and take slaves to the American colonies. This, and the difficulty of travel within the continent, meant that the various peoples of Africa remained isolated from the rest of the world until the present century. There are two main types of African—the Hamites and Semites of the north and the Negroes of south and central Africa.

The Hamites and Semites are so named because they are said to be descendants of the Bible characters Ham and Shem, sons of Noah. They have mixed and traded with Europeans, their neighbours on the far side of the Mediterranean, for thousands of years.

Apart from a few coastal areas, Africa south of the Sahara had little contact with Europeans. The people of these regions are dark-skinned, but there are big differences between the Negroes of different areas. There are also Asians and Europeans living in many parts of Africa. Along with the African races they make up a population of over 350 million.

From the 19th century until the 1950s most countries of Africa were ruled by European nations. Only four were ruled by themselves. Now almost all of the African countries are independent, and they are trying to work together to help each other.

Modern buildings line the streets of Nairobi (above), the capital of Kenya.

African women carry baskets of washing on their heads. The people of Africa, particularly south of the Sahara, are mostly Negroes. They make up about 70 per cent of the total population of Africa.

Children playing outdoors at a school in Nigeria (above). There is a shortage of schools in many parts of Africa but the governments are building new classrooms and training new teachers to help with the problem.

A market in Morocco (left). Most Moroccans make their living on the land, bringing their produce to sell in the markets. The people of Morocco are mainly Arabs (Semites) and Berbers (Hamites), or a mixture of the two.

41

The Wealth of Africa

Much of Africa is not suited to large-scale farming. But modern agricultural methods are now being used to make better use of the land. The most important crops include cotton, sisal, coffee, cocoa, palm trees (for palm oil and kernels to make cosmetics and soap), and peanuts. Vines are grown in Algeria, Morocco, and South Africa. In areas with a tropical climate there are bananas and rubber. Maize is grown in many places, but millet, rice, and wheat are also important. Dates are grown in parts of the Sahara where there is water. Mediterranean plants such as olives, figs, lemons, and oranges grow in the south-west as well as in the far north.

Africa is not very rich in oil and coal although there are important gas and oil deposits in the Sahara and Nigeria. But it does have valuable gold, copper, manganese, phosphate, and diamond mines. South Africa is the main manufacturing centre. But industries are now developing slowly in other parts of the continent.

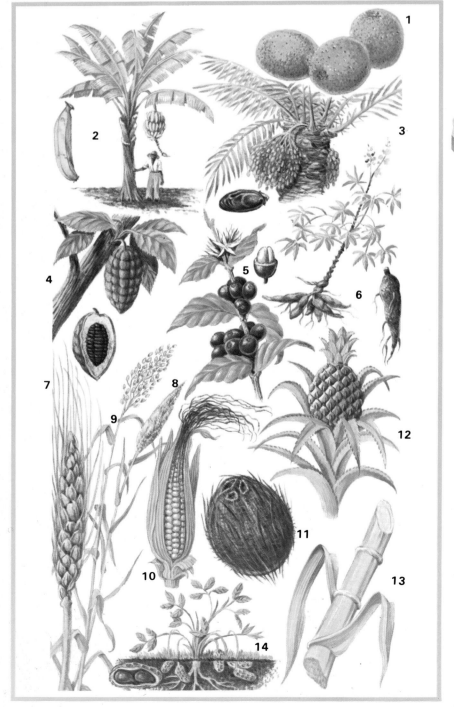

	CROPS				
	Olives		Sugarcane		Dates
	Grapes		Cacao (Cocoa)		Tobacco
	Wheat		Rice		Citrus Fruit
	Coffee		Bananas		Peanuts (Groundnuts)
	Palm Oil		Rubber		Maize
	Sisal		Cotton		Millet and Sorghum

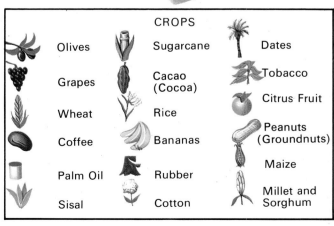

Food Crops (left)
1. Oranges	5. Coffee	10. Maize
2. Bananas	6. Cassava	11. Coconut
3. Dates	7. Wheat	12. Pineapple
4. Cacao (Cocoa)	8. Millet	13. Sugarcane
	9. Sorghum	14. Peanuts

Fishing is important to the people living near the sea and lakes in Africa. Here fishermen set sail on the coast of Kenya.

Cattle are kept in herds by these Masai tribesmen (above left). The Masai wander with their herds over the open grasslands of Kenya in search of good grazing grounds and water.

Diamonds are mined underground. Machines above (right) crush the rock to free the diamonds. These are then sent to factories for cutting and polishing. Diamonds are the most sought after of all the precious stones. South Africa is the world's most important diamond centre.

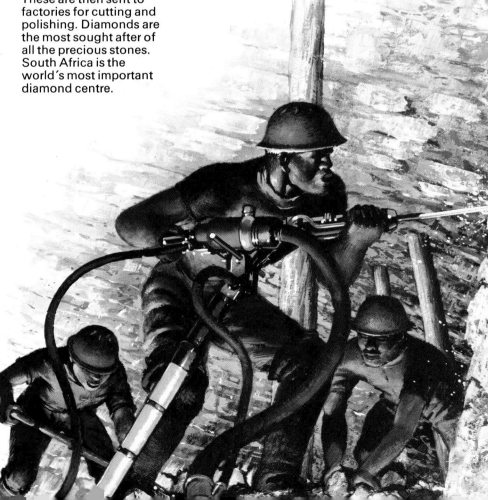

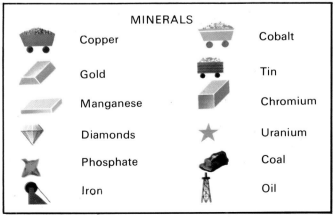

MINERALS

Copper		Cobalt	
Gold		Tin	
Manganese		Chromium	
Diamonds		Uranium	
Phosphate		Coal	
Iron		Oil	

Mining gold in South Africa. The greatest goldfields in the world are found here. A worker bores a hole in the rock before it is packed with explosives. The explosives are used to blast the rock from the mines. The rock is then broken up, crushed, and mixed with water before the gold can be removed from it.

Grey Parrot

Flamingo

White Pelican

Secretary Bird

Hornbill

Carmine Bee-eater

Crowned Crane

African Wildlife

Africa was once the home of countless different animals. But as more and more of the continent became farming land, many of the animals were driven away so that some are threatened with extinction. Luckily, various African governments saw what was happening. Large game reserves and national parks have now been fenced off to protect the animals.

Africa is the home of the largest land animal in the world —the elephant. The African elephant, bigger than his Indian relative, can be as much as three metres in height and weigh up to six tonnes. The tusks alone weigh over a hundred kilogrammes. Another large inhabitant of the continent is the rhinoceros, which also has relations in India. The African rhinoceros has two horns whereas the Indian has only one.

Many members of the cat family live in Africa, the king being the lion. Lions live in large families called prides in open grassland where they hunt zebras, giraffes, antelopes, and other creatures of the savanna. Another large cat found in Africa is the cheetah. The cheetah is yellow with black spots and is the fastest animal over short distances. It can run at speeds of up to 60 kilometres an hour.

Gorillas, chimpanzees, and many different kinds of monkeys have made their homes in the trees of the dense tropical forests. These forests are also rich in birds and insects. The deserts have very little animal life. Only a few hardy creatures, such as the camel and the fennec fox, manage to live there.

The island of Madagascar has several animals and plants that cannot be seen anywhere else in the world. These include the lemur and the tenrec, a strange creature with a bristly coat.

Savanna grasslands cover much of the high rolling plains of Africa. In the dry season the grass is brown and withered, but as soon as the rains come it recovers quickly and grows very high. Near the forests there are some trees and bushes growing among the grass. The umbrella-shaped trees in the picture are called *acacias*. Weaver birds build unusual nests of grass in them, and lions often laze about under them. Elephants, giraffes, and ostriches roam across the wide plains, while zebras and antelopes drink at the waterhole. A marabou stork stands at the edge of the waterhole with a snake in its mouth.

Barbary Ape

Addax

Fennec Fox

Crocodile

Camel

Cheetah

Bushbuck

Colobus Monkey

Hippopotamus

Eland

Hyena

Beisa Oryx

Gorilla

Chimpanzee

Elephant

Giraffe

Leopard

Lion

Okapi

Rhinoceros

Tenrec

Wildebeest

Zebra

Ostrich

Springbok

Impala

Ring-tailed Lemur

Aardvark

Baboon

Jackass Penguin

45

The Americas

The name *America* comes from the name of the Italian explorer Amerigo Vespucci. It was once thought that he was the first to discover this continent.

America is sometimes thought of as two separate continents, North America and South America. The narrow strip of Central America joins the two. America stretches from the Arctic Ocean in the north to the Antarctic Ocean in the south. It is almost 14,500 kilometres long, the longest north to south stretch of land in the world.

In the north-west of the continent is Alaska, the 49th state of America. The Rocky Mountains run from here to northern Mexico. East of the Rockies lie the Great Plains. These are drained by the Mississippi River and bordered on the east by the Appalachian Mountains.

Between North and South America is the rugged mountainous region of Central America. It also includes the islands of the Caribbean Sea. Only a narrow piece of land, an *isthmus*, joins Central America to South America. This isthmus is Panama. Across it has been built a canal linking the Atlantic Ocean with the Pacific.

South America is almost as big as North America. It also has a large chain of mountains, the Andes, running along its western coast, and a large central plain. A big part of the plain is covered in tropical forest and crossed by the mighty Amazon River.

The Great Lakes
The Great Lakes are on the border of Canada and the United States. They are Lakes Superior, Michigan, Huron, Erie, and Ontario. It is possible for a ship to sail from the Atlantic, up the St Lawrence River and across the lakes, right to the heart of the continent. The magnificent Niagara Falls (below) are on the Niagara River between Lake Erie and Lake Ontario.

The Andes and the Amazon
A vast mountain range, the Andes, runs along the full length of the west coast of South America. It stretches in an almost unbroken line for 8000 kilometres, the world's longest mountain range. It has many volcanoes and the whole area is shaken from time to time by severe earthquakes. South American Indians live and farm high up on the grassy areas between the snow-capped peaks.

Other Indians live on the eastern side of the Andes where rivers have carried large amounts of silt down from the mountains. Over millions of years this silt has built up into vast plains. The largest of these plains has been formed by the Amazon River and its tributaries.

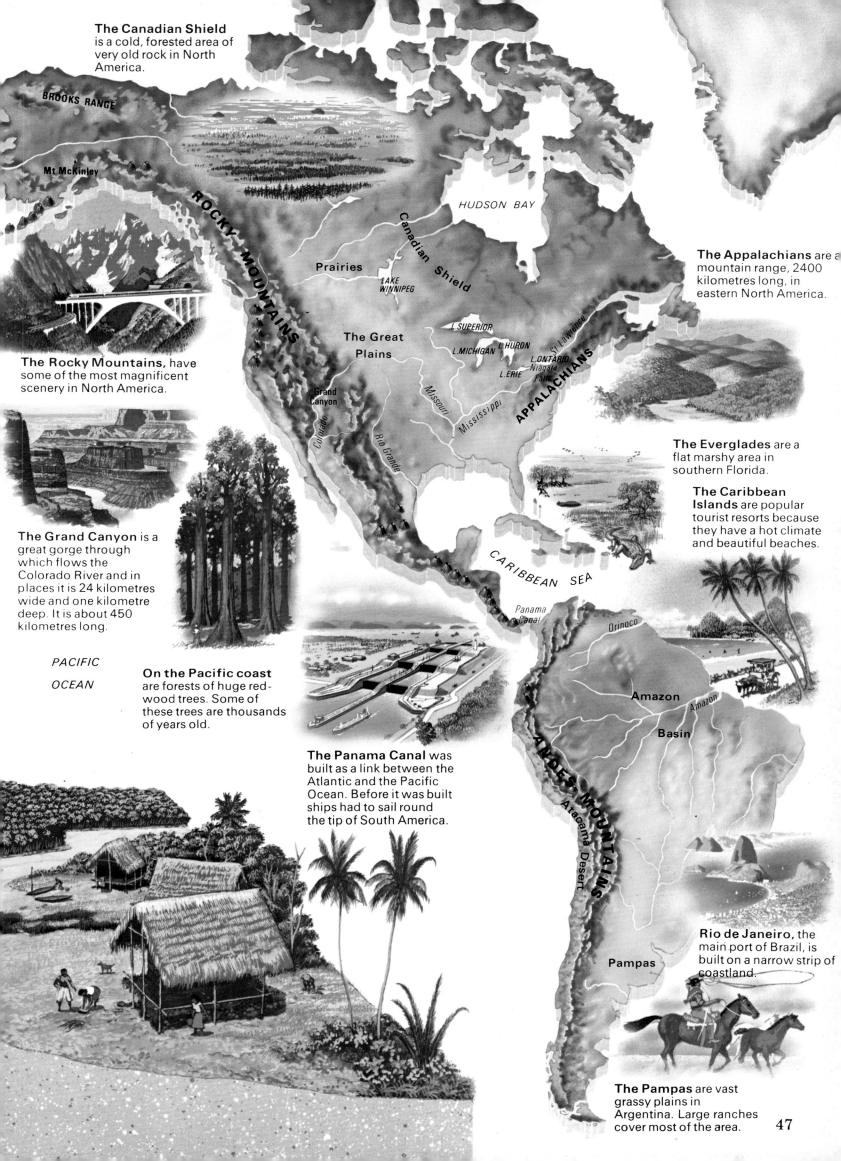

The Canadian Shield is a cold, forested area of very old rock in North America.

BROOKS RANGE

Mt McKinley

ROCKY MOUNTAINS

The Rocky Mountains, have some of the most magnificent scenery in North America.

The Grand Canyon is a great gorge through which flows the Colorado River and in places it is 24 kilometres wide and one kilometre deep. It is about 450 kilometres long.

PACIFIC

OCEAN

On the Pacific coast are forests of huge red-wood trees. Some of these trees are thousands of years old.

The Panama Canal was built as a link between the Atlantic and the Pacific Ocean. Before it was built ships had to sail round the tip of South America.

HUDSON BAY

Prairies

Canadian Shield

LAKE WINNIPEG

The Great Plains

L.SUPERIOR

L.MICHIGAN

L.HURON

St Lawrence

L.ONTARIO
Niagara Falls

L.ERIE

APPALACHIANS

Grand Canyon

Colorado

Rio Grande

Missouri

Mississippi

The Appalachians are a mountain range, 2400 kilometres long, in eastern North America.

The Everglades are a flat marshy area in southern Florida.

The Caribbean Islands are popular tourist resorts because they have a hot climate and beautiful beaches.

CARIBBEAN SEA

Panama Canal

Orinoco

Amazon

Amazon Basin

ANDES MOUNTAINS

Atacama Desert

Rio de Janeiro, the main port of Brazil, is built on a narrow strip of coastland.

Pampas

The Pampas are vast grassy plains in Argentina. Large ranches cover most of the area.

47

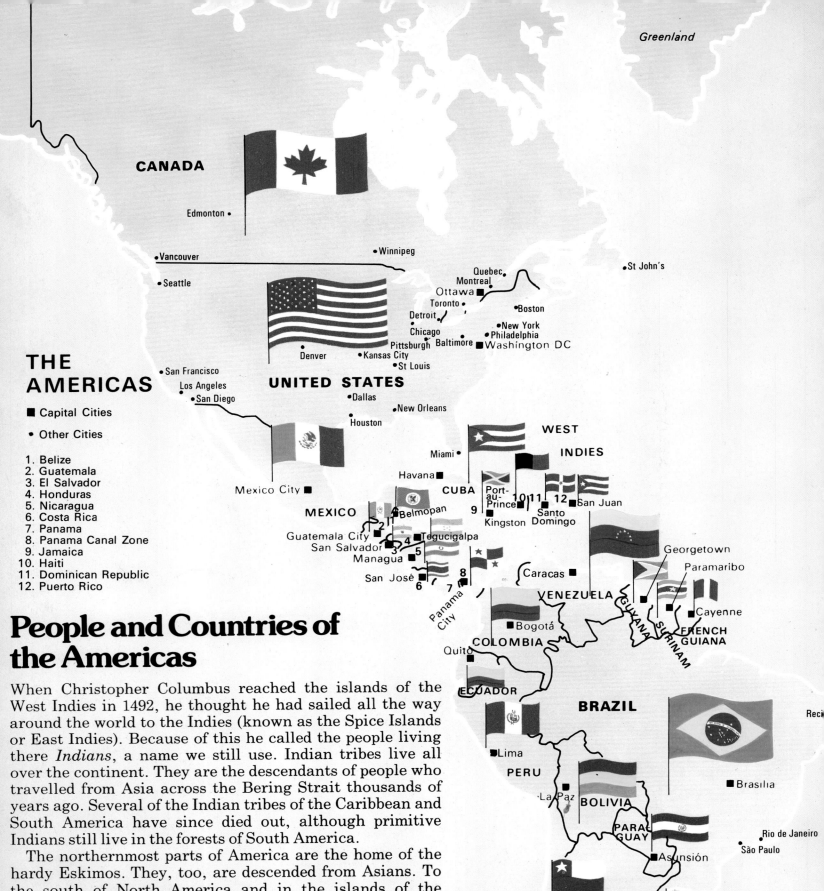

CANADA

Edmonton

THE AMERICAS

■ Capital Cities

• Other Cities

1. Belize
2. Guatemala
3. El Salvador
4. Honduras
5. Nicaragua
6. Costa Rica
7. Panama
8. Panama Canal Zone
9. Jamaica
10. Haiti
11. Dominican Republic
12. Puerto Rico

Greenland

Vancouver • • Winnipeg

Seattle •

Quebec •
Montreal •
Ottawa ■
Toronto •
Detroit •
Chicago •
Pittsburgh • Baltimore •
Denver • • Kansas City
• St Louis

• St John's

• Boston
• New York
• Philadelphia
■ Washington DC

San Francisco •
Los Angeles •
• San Diego

UNITED STATES

• Dallas
Houston •
• New Orleans

Miami •

WEST INDIES

Havana ■

CUBA

Mexico City ■

MEXICO

Belmopan ■
Guatemala City ■
San Salvador ■
Managua ■
San José ■

Port-au-Prince ■
Kingston ■
Santo Domingo ■
San Juan ■

Tegucigalpa ■

9

Caracas ■

VENEZUELA

Bogotá ■

COLOMBIA

Quito ■

Panama City

Georgetown
Paramaribo
Cayenne

GUYANA
SURINAM
FRENCH GUIANA

ECUADOR

Lima ■

PERU

BRAZIL

Brasília ■

Recife

La Paz ■

BOLIVIA

PARAGUAY

Asunción ■

Rio de Janeiro
São Paulo

Santiago ■

CHILE

ARGENTINA

Buenos Aires ■

URUGUAY

Montevideo ■

People and Countries of the Americas

When Christopher Columbus reached the islands of the West Indies in 1492, he thought he had sailed all the way around the world to the Indies (known as the Spice Islands or East Indies). Because of this he called the people living there *Indians*, a name we still use. Indian tribes live all over the continent. They are the descendants of people who travelled from Asia across the Bering Strait thousands of years ago. Several of the Indian tribes of the Caribbean and South America have since died out, although primitive Indians still live in the forests of South America.

The northernmost parts of America are the home of the hardy Eskimos. They, too, are descended from Asians. To the south of North America and in the islands of the Caribbean there are many blacks. They are descendants of slaves brought over from Africa.

But most of the people of modern America came originally from Europe. Their families went to America in the hope of finding a better life than they had in their own countries. In North America these people are of mainly British, French, Dutch, and German origin. In Central and South America the people are mainly of Spanish and Portuguese descent.

North America, with a population of over 330 million, has only three countries: Canada, the United States, and Mexico. South America, on the other hand, with a smaller population of around 200 million, is a land of many separate countries.

Skyscrapers in Manhattan, New York City. New York is the largest city in America and, after Tokyo in Japan, is the second largest in the world.

Sport plays an important part in American life. Football, a tough and exciting game, is the most popular autumn sport in the United States.

A market in Ecuador. Indians from different villages gather in the market to sell their local crops and products.

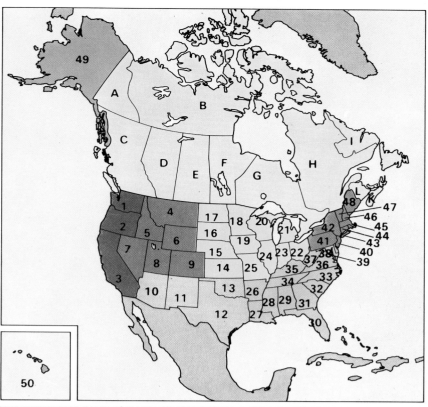

THE STATES OF NORTH AMERICA

STATE	CAPITAL	STATE	CAPITAL
Pacific Coast States		**Southern States**	
1. Washington	Olympia	26. Arkansas	Little Rock
2. Oregon	Salem	27. Louisiana	Baton Rouge
3. California	Sacramento	28. Mississippi	Jackson
		29. Alabama	Montgomery
Rocky Mountain States		30. Florida	Tallahassee
4. Montana	Helena	31. Georgia	Atlanta
5. Idaho	Boise	32. South Carolina	Columbia
6. Wyoming	Cheyenne	33. North Carolina	Raleigh
7. Nevada	Carson City	34. Tennessee	Nashville
8. Utah	Salt Lake City	35. Kentucky	Frankfort
9. Colorado	Denver	36. Virginia	Richmond
		37. West Virginia	Charleston
South-western States		38. Maryland	Annapolis
10. Arizona	Phoenix	39. Delaware	Dover
11. New Mexico	Sante Fe		
12. Texas	Austin	**Mid-Atlantic States**	
13. Oklahoma	Oklahoma City	40. New Jersey	Trenton
		41. Pennsylvania	Harrisburg
Mid-western States		42. New York	Albany
14. Kansas	Topeka		
15. Nebraska	Lincoln	**New England**	
16. South Dakota	Pierre	43. Connecticut	Hartford
17. North Dakota	Bismarck	44. Rhode Island	Providence
18. Minnesota	St Paul	45. Massachusetts	Boston
19. Iowa	Des Moines	46. Vermont	Montpelier
20. Wisconsin	Madison	47. New Hampshire	Concord
21. Michigan	Lansing	48. Maine	Augusta
22. Ohio	Columbus		
23. Indiana	Indianapolis		
24. Illinois	Springfield	49. Alaska	Juneau
25. Missouri	Jefferson City	50. Hawaii	Honolulu

THE PROVINCES AND TERRITORIES OF CANADA

A.	Yukon Territory	Whitehorse	G.	Ontario	Toronto
B.	Northwest		H.	Quebec	Quebec
	Territories	Yellowknife	I.	Newfoundland	St John's
C.	British Columbia	Victoria	J.	Prince Edward	
D.	Alberta	Edmonton		Island	Charlottetown
E.	Saskatchewan	Regina	K.	Nova Scotia	Halifax
F.	Manitoba	Winnipeg	L.	New Brunswick	Fredericton

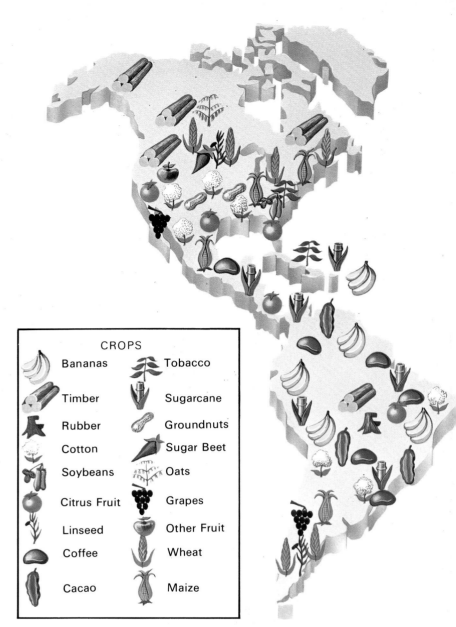

CROPS

Bananas	Tobacco
Timber	Sugarcane
Rubber	Groundnuts
Cotton	Sugar Beet
Soybeans	Oats
Citrus Fruit	Grapes
Linseed	Other Fruit
Coffee	Wheat
Cacao	Maize

Wheat (top) is grown in vast farms on the prairies of North America. It is harvested by machines called *combines*.

Cotton (above) is an important crop in the southern states of the United States, which is the world's leading cotton-growing country.

Cattle (below) are reared on large ranches in the pampas regions of Argentina.

The Wealth of America

Although the wide areas of mountain in North America are not really suitable for farming, huge forests grow there and supply valuable timber. Salmon fishing and the canning of the fish are also big industries in the mountainous regions of the north-west.

The wide open prairies of Canada and the Great Plains of the United States have been called the 'bread basket' of the world because they produce vast quantities of wheat. Canada also has large dairy farms. Brazil is famous for its coffee; Argentina for its cattle; Jamaica for its sugar; and the southern states of the United States for their tobacco and cotton.

Oil, coal, and iron are found throughout the Americas. Gold, silver, copper, nickel, and several other metals are also mined. The United States is the world's leading producer of zinc and copper; Mexico mines the most silver; Canada the most nickel; and Jamaica is the leading supplier of bauxite which is used to make aluminium.

Manufacturing industries in North America are centred in the large cities, such as Detroit and Pittsburgh. Industry is not very well developed in South America, although in recent years it has been growing rapidly.

MINERALS

Bauxite	Oil
Copper	Coal
Iron	Nickel
Lead	Tin
Zinc	Sulphur
Manganese	Phosphate
Silver	Emeralds
Gold	Diamonds

Copper is mined in Chile at Chuquicamata, the largest open cast mine in the world. Chile is the world's leading copper producer.

Oil is produced in huge quantities in the Americas and it is one of their most valuable exports. These derricks are used to drill deep into the ground for oil.

Molten Iron is poured into a furnace in an iron and steel foundry in Hamilton, Canada. The production of iron and steel is most important to Canada's wealth. Iron and steel are the cheapest and most widely used metals in the world. Thousands of things that surround us in our daily lives are made from them. They include bridges, ships, cars, machinery, bicycles, furniture, refrigerators, wire, nails, and tin cans.

American Wildlife

The animals of North America vary from the caribou and polar bears of the cold north to the alligators and colourful parrots of the tropical south. In the wooded areas between are bears, moose, deer, chipmunks, porcupines, raccoons, and beavers.

Different animals live in the grassland areas. Beneath the prairies there are lots of small tunnels—a cause of lots of problems to farmers. Responsible for digging the tunnels are marmots, squirrel-like creatures sometimes called *prairie dogs* because they make a barking noise. Their main enemies are black-footed ferrets, badgers, and coyotes. The most famous animal of the prairies is the bison, or buffalo, as Americans call it. At one time great herds of bison roamed the plains, but the Indians and the settlers killed so many that these animals are now protected. Another creature of the prairies and desert is the rattlesnake. It is so called because it has loose bones in its tail that make a noise like a baby's rattle when it is alarmed.

South America is the home of giant worms, monster moths, and poisonous frogs. But the most unusual animal of all is the giant armadillo. Its back is covered with bony-plated bands, rather like a knight's armour. It feeds on insects, and uses its strong claws to rip open ants' nests. It then pushes in its long sticky tongue and eats the ants— just like the giant anteater that lives in the same area. Another strange animal is the sloth which moves very slowly indeed. The sloth spends a lot of its time hanging upside down in the trees of the Amazon rain forest.

This Amazon rain forest is also the home of lots of snakes. King of these snakes is the boa which can be as much as nine metres long. It is not a poisonous snake, but it kills its prey by crushing it with its powerful body. The anaconda, a relative of the boa, also lives in the forests. Another inhabitant of this area is the tapir, a strange creature about the size of a pony, but it has a short trunk and thick hairy skin. In the trees a wealth of brightly coloured birds, including parrots, toucans and hummingbirds, are found feeding on the fruit and nectar. And in the rivers there are many different kinds of fish, including the dreaded piranha.

The toucan (above) has a large, colourful beak which it uses to push through the leaves to reach fruit and berries in the tropical forests of South America.

The moose (top) lives in the cold northern forests of North America. It spends most of the summer feeding on water plants in and around lakes.

The piranha (above centre) is a ferocious fish that lives in the rivers of the Amazon rain forest. Its teeth are so sharp that it can cut flesh as neatly as a razor.

Bison (right) roam over the grasslands of North America. Today there are only a few herds left in the wild.

Caribou

Grizzly Bear

Canada Goose

Rocky Mountain Goat

Lynx

Skunk

Beaver

Chipmunk

Porcupine

Raccoon

White-tailed Deer

Rattlesnake

Bison

Pronghorn

Prairie Dog

Alligator

California Sea-lion

Coyote

Solenodon

Horned Toad

Opossum

Giant Turtle

Howler Monkey

Vampire Bat

Parrot

Marmoset

Capybara

Hummingbird

Sloth

Llama

Jaguar

Vicuna

Tapir

Giant Anteater

Chinchilla

Nine-banded Armadillo

Condor

Rhea

BALD EAGLE

Oceania

Oceania is the name of a group of islands in the south and central Pacific Ocean. The biggest of these islands, Australia, is also the largest island in the world but the smallest continent. Much of Australia has broad plains and a few low mountain ranges. The middle is all desert.

Australia was unknown to Europeans until the 17th century. It was thought that there was land in this area but no-one knew for certain. People called this mystery continent *Terra Australis Incognita*, which means 'the unknown land of the south'. Dutch sailors were the first to discover it, but it was not until a hundred years later that Captain James Cook mapped part of the east coast of the continent accurately.

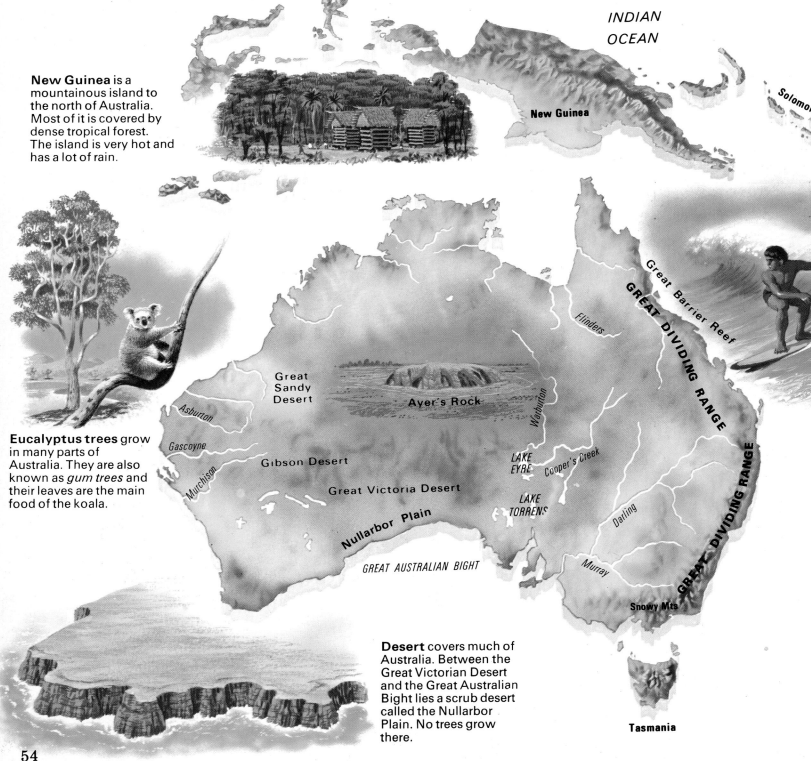

New Guinea is a mountainous island to the north of Australia. Most of it is covered by dense tropical forest. The island is very hot and has a lot of rain.

INDIAN OCEAN

New Guinea

Solomon Is

Eucalyptus trees grow in many parts of Australia. They are also known as *gum trees* and their leaves are the main food of the koala.

Great Barrier Reef

GREAT DIVIDING RANGE

Flinders

Great Sandy Desert

Ayer's Rock

Warburton

Asburton

Gascoyne

Murchison

Gibson Desert

LAKE EYRE

Cooper's Creek

Great Victoria Desert

LAKE TORRENS

Darling

Nullarbor Plain

GREAT AUSTRALIAN BIGHT

Murray

GREAT DIVIDING RANGE

Snowy Mts

Desert covers much of Australia. Between the Great Victorian Desert and the Great Australian Bight lies a scrub desert called the Nullarbor Plain. No trees grow there.

Tasmania

Asia

Australasia

Antarctic

The second largest country in Oceania is New Zealand. In addition to the North and the South Islands this country also includes Stewart Island, Chatham Island, and several smaller islands. The land is very different from that of Australia. There are many mountains, glaciers, volcanoes, and geysers. Rainfall is heavier and the climate is generally more temperate. Much of the country was once forest, but a great deal has been cleared. A lot of this clearing was done by the Maoris. They are brown-skinned people who were living in New Zealand when the first white people came to the islands. They used to burn the forests so often that the early explorers called New Zealand *Smoke Land*. The first European to visit New Zealand was the Dutch explorer Abel Janszoon Tasman in 1642. Although other Europeans started arriving in the years that followed, the country was still unexplored until 1850.

Islands and Atolls

Much of Oceania consists of small islands. Some of the islands have been made by volcanoes. There are so many volcanoes around the Pacific Ocean that it is often called *the ring of fire.* Most of the islands formed in this way are mountainous.

Other islands are flat and made of coral —the skeletons of tiny sea creatures. These islands are called *atolls.* They are only found in the warm south seas. The Great Barrier Reef off the coast of north-east Australia is the largest mass of coral in the world.

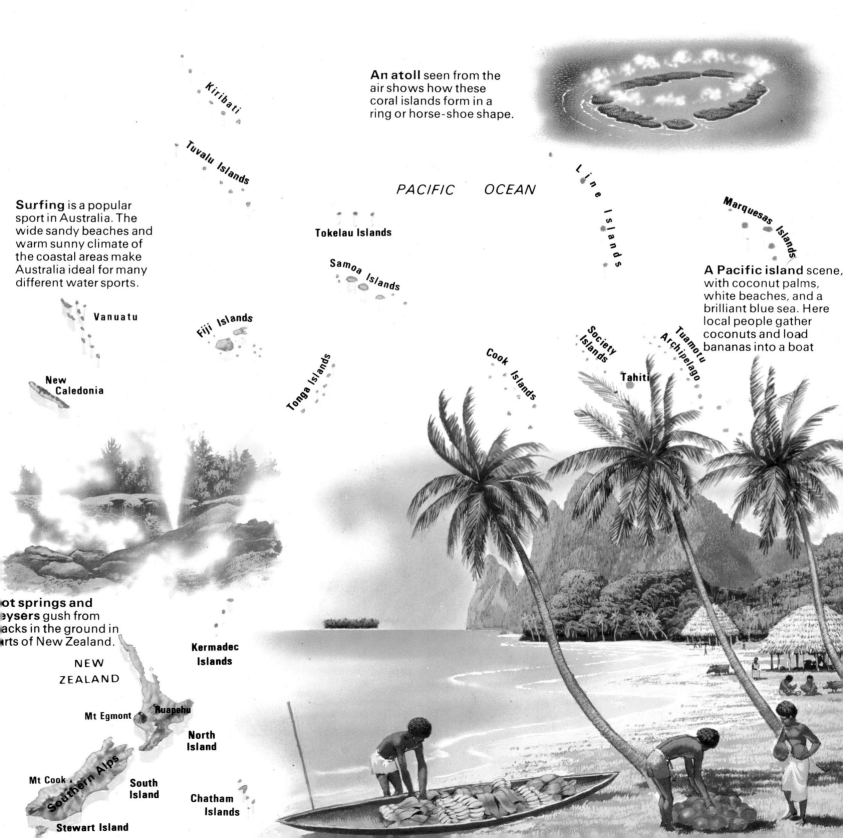

An atoll seen from the air shows how these coral islands form in a ring or horse-shoe shape.

Kiribati

Tuvalu Islands

PACIFIC OCEAN

Line Islands

Marquesas Islands

Tokelau Islands

Surfing is a popular sport in Australia. The wide sandy beaches and warm sunny climate of the coastal areas make Australia ideal for many different water sports.

Samoa Islands

A Pacific island scene, with coconut palms, white beaches, and a brilliant blue sea. Here local people gather coconuts and load bananas into a boat

Vanuatu

Fiji Islands

Society Islands

Tuamotu Archipelago

Cook Islands

New Caledonia

Tonga Islands

Tahiti

ot springs and eysers gush from acks in the ground in rts of New Zealand.

Kermadec Islands

NEW ZEALAND

Mt Egmont   Ruapehu

North Island

Mt Cook   Southern Alps

South Island

Chatham Islands

Stewart Island

The People and Wealth of Oceania

The islands of Oceania are sometimes grouped according to the type of people who live on them. These are *Melanesia*, *Micronesia*, and *Polynesia*. The people of Melanesia are very much like the Negroes of Africa, whereas the people of Micronesia are a mixture between the people of Melanesia and those of Polynesia.

The best-known Polynesian people are the Maoris of New Zealand. It is thought that they either came from Asia or, more probably, from South America. The natives of Australia are the Aborigines. Some Aborigines still live the simple lives of their forefathers, but many now work on farms and in towns.

The total population of Oceania is just over 18 million—really very small when compared with the rest of the world. Thirteen million people live in Australia, but because so much is desert, over half of them live in a small area in the south-east. Many of these people are of European origin. Some are the descendants of British convicts who were sent to Australia in the 18th and 19th centuries. When gold was discovered in 1851, thousands of other people settled in the continent.

Today, Australia has a wealth of resources besides gold, including silver, copper, lead, zinc, and nickel. Sheep farming is the most important industry in both Australia and New Zealand. Beef cattle are also important, as are wheat farming and fruit growing. Butter and cheese are also valuable exports of New Zealand.

Sydney is the largest city in Australia. The harbour bridge and the unusual sail-like domes of the new opera house are clearly seen from the air.

Wellington, the capital of New Zealand, lies in steep hills that surround the harbour.

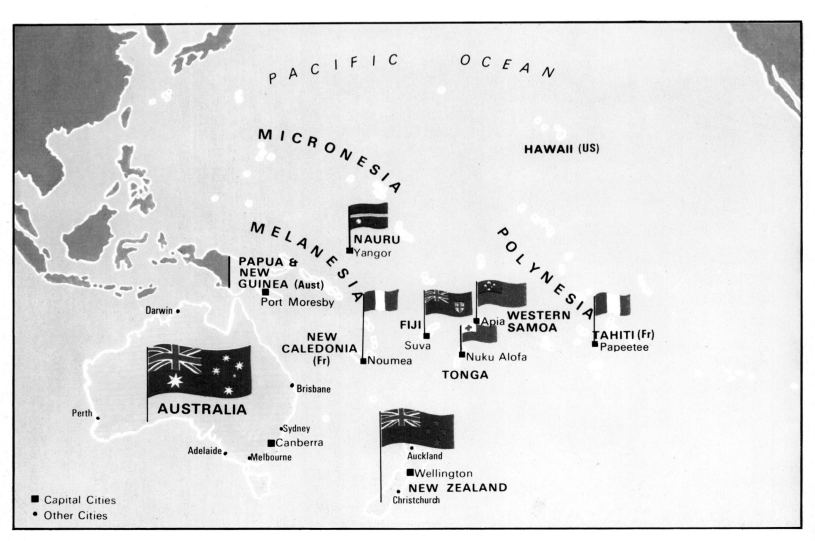

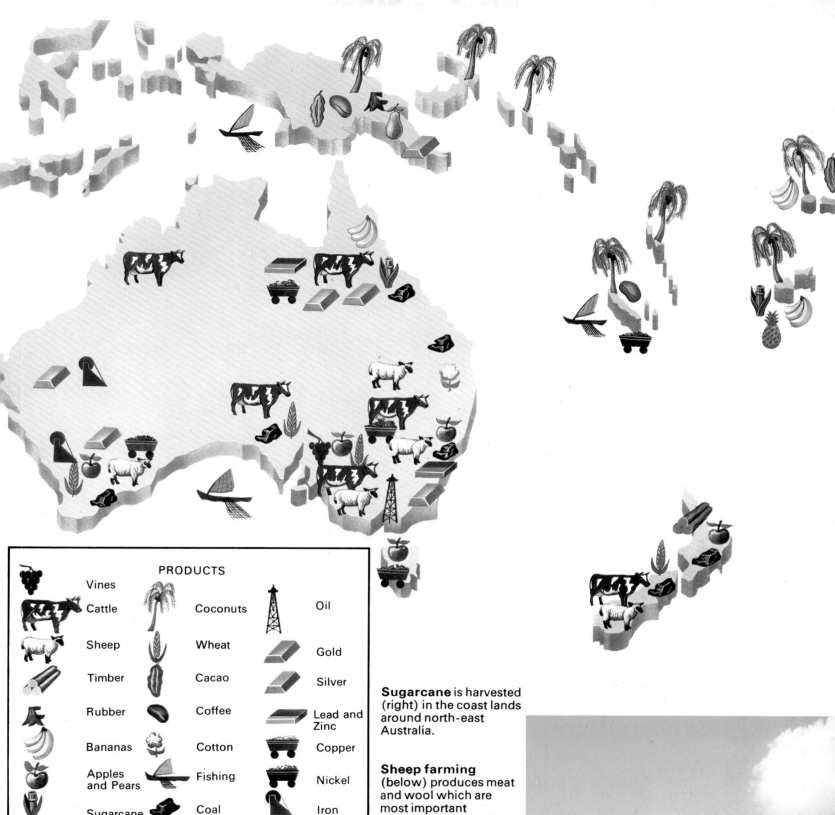

PRODUCTS

Vines	Coconuts	Oil
Cattle	Wheat	Gold
Sheep	Cacao	Silver
Timber	Coffee	Lead and Zinc
Rubber	Cotton	Copper
Bananas	Fishing	Nickel
Apples and Pears	Coal	Iron
Sugarcane		

Sugarcane is harvested (right) in the coast lands around north-east Australia.

Sheep farming (below) produces meat and wool which are most important industries in Australia and New Zealand.

Wildlife of Oceania

Oceania has many creatures that are found nowhere else in the world. Only in Australia can you see the koala, a brown woolly animal that lives on eucalyptus leaves. It never drinks and the name *koala*, from the Aborigine language, means *nothing to drink*. Australia's best known animal is the kangaroo. A full grown kangaroo is about two metres high and weighs 90 kilogrammes. It can leap nine metres and jump obstacles three metres high. One of the world's largest birds, the emu, lives in Australia. The emu cannot fly but it can run very fast. Other flightless birds of Oceania include the cassowary, the curious kiwi of New Zealand, and the takahe, a brightly coloured parrot.

Possibly the strangest animal in this continent of weird and wonderful creatures is the platypus. It has a bill like a duck, a tail like a beaver, a furry body, and webbed feet with claws. It lives in burrows, but is just as at home in water. When it swims it keeps its eyes closed and cannot see where it is going!

The koala bear of Australia is not a bear but a marsupial. Marsupials are animals that carry their newborn young around in a pouch until they are old enough to look after themselves. Kangaroos are also marsupials.

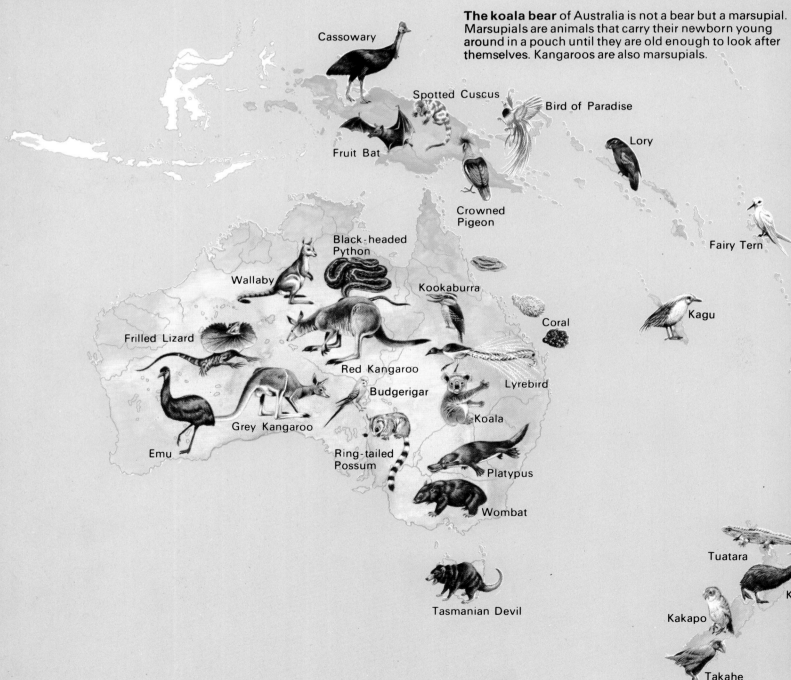

Index

ACKNOWLEDGEMENTS

Picture Research: PENNY WARN and JACKIE NEWTON

Cover: ROY COOMBS

Artwork: Graham Allen 28-29, 36-37, 44 *top*, 45, 53, 58; Norman Barber 14-15; Roy Coombs 6, 7, 9, 10-11, 12-13, 20-21, 22-23, 26 *bottom*, 30-31, 38-39, 43 *bottom*, 46-47, 51 *bottom*, 54-55; Shireen Faircloth 16-17, 18-19, 41, 42 *left*; Richard Orr 44 *bottom*; Mike Saunders 26 *top*, 27, 34, 35, 42 *right*, 43 *left*, 50, 51 *top*; George Thompson back endpaper; Brian Watson front end paper, 25, 32-33, 40, 48, 56.

Photographs: Australian News & Information Bureau 56 *top*, 57, 58; Martin Borland 46, 49 *top*; British Steel 51 *centre*; Camera and Pen International 51 *top*; Michael Chinery 29 *centre*; Dave Collins 15 *bottom*, 32 *centre*, 41 *centre top*; FIAT 27 *bottom*; Finnish Tourist Board 27 *centre*; French Government Tourist Office 26; Japan Information Centre 32 *top*; London Tin Corporation Ltd 35 *bottom right*; National Panasonic 35 *top*; National Tourist Office of Italy 24 *centre right*; Natural History Photographic Agency 42, 52 *top*, *centre top*, *bottom*; New Zealand High Commission 56 *centre*; Royal Netherlands Tourist Office 24 *top*; Satour 43 *centre*; ZEFA 24 *centre left*, *bottom left*, 27 *top*, 30, 34 *top*, 35 *bottom left*, 41 *top*, *bottom*, 43 *top*, 50 *top*.

The publishers wish to thank Trevor Marchington and Peter Eldin for their kind assistance in the preparation of this book.

GREENLAND

BRITISH
ISLES

NORTH
AMERICA

ATLANTIC

OCEAN

PACIFIC

OCEAN

CENTRAL
AMERICA

Caribbean Sea

SOUTH
AMERICA